Homebrew Classics

India Pale Ale

Clive La Pensée
& Roger Protz

The authentic history of India Pale Ale.
Recipes from the past made ready for you to
brew at home.

BOOKS

Homebrew Classics

Authors: Clive La Pensée and Roger Protz

Cover design by Rob Howells

Cover photography by Thomas Dobbie

Printed by WS Bookwell, Finland

Published by CAMRA, The Campaign for Real Ale, 230 Hatfield Road, St. Albans, Herts AL1 4LW

Managing Editor: Mark Webb, mark-webb@msn.com

© CAMRA Ltd 2001

ISBN 1-85249-129-9

CONTENTS

Introduction

This is a new kind of book for beer enthusiasts. Between its covers you will find a wealth of information about the particular brewing style of India Pale Ale (IPA). You will also find recipes and instructions to help you brew your own IPA, with as much authenticity and/or creativity that you wish to employ.

Roger Protz's history of how IPA came about is a fascinating, almost cinematic, visit to breweries, warehouses, ships and offices of the 18th and 19th centuries. He also tells the tale of how, in the 20th century, the style of IPA has been revived and has come to be revered by some brewers and beer lovers.

Clive La Pensée gives us the reality of brewing IPA, the very ingredients, temperatures and timings that produced, and now reproduce, the beer known as India Pale Ale. His recipes are like the notes of a detective on the trail of a missing person. Reading them, and brewing with them, makes you part of the story.

Welcome to a new kind of book – the Homebrew Classics. Look out for other titles in the series on *Stout & Porter, Mild, Bitter,* and other famous beer styles.

India Pale Ale
from revolution to revival

by *Roger Protz*

So we beat on, boats against the current, borne back ceaselessly into the past
— F Scott Fitzgerald: The Great Gatsby

**Bow Bridge, East London, in the 1830s,
with Hodgson's Brewery on the right.**

ndia Pale Ale is a paradox. It was a revolutionary beer style that transformed brewing on a world scale. It not only pre-dated lager brewing by several decades but also inspired the first producers of cold-fermented beers in Central Europe. It marked a decisive break with the past: porter and stout had been the first truly commercial beers but their methods of production were a compromise between the new technologies of the Industrial Revolution and older practices reaching back into rural, feudal times. The pale ale brewers grasped new technology eagerly. They made use of steam power, improved malting, mashing and copper boiling, refrigeration to cool and store beer, and a scientific understanding of the role of yeast in fermentation. British brewers at the turn of the 18th and 19th centuries were bold innovators, their attitudes moulded by the first fully-fledged capitalist system that dominated the world, acquired enormous wealth, and restlessly searched for new markets and improved methods of production. As the social historian Eric Hobsbawm wrote in Industry and Empire (1968): "The Industrial Revolution marks the most fundamental transformation of human life in the history of the world recorded in written documents.

For a brief period it coincided with the history of a single country, Great Britain. An entire world economy was thus built on, or rather around, Britain, and this country therefore temporarily rose to a position of global influence and power unparalleled by any state of its relative size before or since, and unlikely to be paralleled by any state in the foreseeable future. There was a moment in the world's history when Britain can be described, if we are not too pedantic, as its only workshop, its only massive importer and exporter, its only carrier, its only imperialist, almost its only foreign investor." British brewers were in the vanguard of this profound social and economic metamorphosis. While the first lager beers in Bavaria were dark and their brewers tentative modernisers until golden Pilsner appeared in neighbouring Bohemia, pale ale brewers proudly proclaimed: "This is new!" and set out to conquer the world with it.

Yet the life of India Pale Ale, in its first manifestation, was comparatively brief. It was born at the end of the 18th century and, to all intents and purposes, was dead a century later. It was supplanted at home by less aggressively potent pale ales and bitters, and internationally by lager beers as Germany and later the United States began to challenge the hegemony of Britain as the world's leading manufacturing power. But the legacy of IPA lived on. It acted as a leitmotif for the theory and practice of brewing in Britain. And it was reborn towards the end of the 20th century as brewers in both Britain and the United States researched the roots of the world's great beer styles and began to recreate them with enormous verve and dedication.

The fact that lager beer accounts for 93 per cent of all the beer brewed in the world today tends to mask the catalytic importance of India Pale Ale. The scientific developments of the 19th century did not influence lager brewing alone. Inspired by the work of Louis Pasteur, British brewers added laboratories, employed chemists, inspected their yeast strains through microscopes, and weeded out bad strains that impeded good fermentation.

They installed cast-iron mash tuns that held the heat better than wood, were far larger (holding up to 200,000 gallons of the sugary extract known as wort) and had longer life spans. Mashing was made more effective and the temperature of the milled malt (grist) and "liquor" (water) was maintained by mechanical pre-mashing devices. Steam-driven rakes stirred the mash, releasing horses from the toil of plodding endlessly round the tuns to turn the rakes. In the middle of the 19th century, Scottish brewers developed the method known as "sparging", from the French *asperger*, to sprinkle: the spent or used grains were mechanically sprayed with hot liquor to wash out any remaining malt sugars at the end of the mashing stage. Sparging put paid to the old system of producing three or four beers of decreasing strength from the same mash. As a result, mash tuns could be utilised more effectively and profitably by pushing through new brews every few hours.

Coppers, fired by coal or coke, were turned from open pans into enclosed domed vessels that avoided heat loss and retained the essential aromas of the hops. Large pans called cool ships, where the hopped wort cooled prior to fermentation, were replaced by heat exchange units: the liquid was pumped through pipes or plates that alternated with pipes holding running cold water. The wort was no longer open to the atmosphere and was free from the risk of infection from wild yeasts and bacteria. When ice-making machines were invented, they were embraced with as much enthusiasm in Britain as they were in Bavaria.

The removal of tax on glass led to the rapid replacement of pewter drinking tankards by cheaper, mass-produced glasses. Drinkers could see their beer and were unimpressed by the murky nature of brown ales and porters. The brewers of pale ale now had a large domestic market at their disposal and developed new fermenting vessels that produced clear, sparkling beers and which proved fundamental to the taste and character of IPA and pale ale. In Burton-on-Trent, which rapidly became the epicentre of pale-ale brewing, the "union set", large oak casks linked together (or "held in union", to use the quaint Victorian expression) by pipes and troughs, cleansed the fermenting beer of yeast. As the wort fermented, it gushed up pipes from the casks to troughs above. The troughs, or balm trays as they are known in Burton, were held at a slight incline: the liquid ran down the troughs and back via more pipes into the casks while most of the yeast was retained.

The Burton "union set" produced clear, sparkling beers that caught the drinking trend of the times.

A growing demand for pale ale, in particular from the burgeoning ranks of the new middle class that refused to contemplate the dark beers of the hoi-polloi, encouraged brewers throughout the country to install their own union sets or to develop other methods of cleansing yeast from their pale ales.

The determinedly independent Yorkshire brewers developed their own system, the Yorkshire square. Still in use at Black Sheep, Samuel Smith and Tetley, the square is a two-storey vessel. The wort is pumped from the bottom storey into the top one through a port hole with a raised edge: the wort runs back into the bottom storey while the yeast is held back by the flange of the port hole. A further development was the "dropping system", still in place at Brakspear of Henley-on-Thames. The fermenters are ranged on two floors. Fermentation starts in the vessels on the first floor. After a few days, the bases of the vessels are opened, and the fermenting wort drains into the vessels below, leaving dead yeast cells and other detritus behind.

There were only two remaining links with the past: the first pale ales were stored for several months, and brewers continued to use yeast strains that worked at warm temperatures. But storage was a response to the colonial trade, not a misty-eyed hankering after the older practice of vatting beer for months or even years: beer destined for India travelled for three

8

months in casks in the holds of sailing ships. And brewers had no intention of moving to cold fermentation and the different type of yeast this involved. Lager brewing was dismissed as a continental irrelevance by men certain of their place at the heart of the greatest empire the world had known since Roman times. In the late 19th century, Bass was arguably the most famous name throughout the lands governed by the British. *The British Mercury* in 1879 described Bass as "a mercantile colossus that has o'erstrided every similar institution in England, if not the world...a monument to the energy of men." *Vanity Fair* in 1871 thought, with misplaced hyperbole, that Michael Thomas Bass's name would be "remembered with gratitude when they [Gladstone and Disraeli] are utterly forgotten." The quality of the new pale ales combined with imperial pride ensured that lager beer made only a fleeting appearance in Victorian England. Lager was seen as a German beer style, a fact that limited its popularity. In Charles Chaplin's film Limelight the following exchange takes place between two music-hall musicians: "Do you know Handel's Largo?" "Yes, but I'd rather have a brown ale!"

Bass was not the only brewery to imprint itself on the consciousness of beer drinkers. Charles Stuart Calverley's famous piece of mid-19th century doggerel was indicative of the fame of the new brewers:

O Beer: O Hodgson, Guinness, Allsopp, Bass!
Names that should be on every infant's tongue!
Shall days and months and years and centuries pass,
And still your merits be unrecked, unsung?

With the obvious exception of Guinness, all the brewers listed made pale ale. It is significant that Hodgson still merited mention alongside the great Burton brewers Allsopp and Bass. For the story of India Pale Ale begins not in Burton-on-Trent but in the premises of an East London brewery, Abbot & Hodgson's Bow Brewery at Bromley-by-Bow, then in the county of Middlesex. In their monumental work, *The British Brewing Industry 1830-1980*, Gourvish and Wilson say that little is known about this "otherwise unremarkable firm", which tends to underestimate both its importance and size.

George Hodgson and his son Mark were brash entrepreneurs who grasped the opportunity to sell beer to the captive British market in India. Before the arrival of good road and rail transport that enabled beer to move easily around the country, the Hodgsons enjoyed pole position in London with their brewery at Bow Bridge.

Bow Brewery in the 1920s.

It stood close to the River Lea that flowed into the Thames alongside the East India Dock Basin, as well the Grand Union Canal, an important conduit for the delivery of malt from Hertford and Ware. Grain would also have been supplied to a neighbouring distillery, whose handsome buildings still stand at Bow Creek by the District Line of the Underground between Bromley-by-Bow and West Ham stations. Hodgson's Brewery was established in 1751 and may have been connected with Hodgson's Kingston Brewery at Kingston upon Thames in Surrey, founded around 1610. George Hodgson, who died in 1814, learned that sailing ships left the East India Docks half-empty and returned with valuable cargoes of spices and silks that covered the costs of the voyages. Rates for cargo on the outward journeys were low. Hodgson heard from his contacts in the docks that soldiers and civilians in India were dissatisfied with

10

exported brown ales, porters and stout. He negotiated special rates for sending his own beer to India and then set about formulating an ale that would suit the perspiring and thirsty colonists.

In the 1780s Hodgson produced a pale ale that for a time established him as a monopoly supplier of the style to the colony. No records exist, but as far as is known, Hodgson called his beer India Ale and did not use the term "pale". But his success with the style and the fact that the Burton brewers deliberately copied his beer suggests it was genuinely pale in colour. The colour of genuine IPAs has become a contentious issue. Many experts argue that the early versions of the style were pale only in comparison to London's brown ales, porters and stouts. The American craft brewer Thom Tomlinson, who brewed an IPA in the 1990s called Renegade Red, suggested in the journal *Brewing Techniques* that Hodgson's India Ale was "copper coloured or reddish bronze". Unless Thom had access to Dr Who's Tardis, he had no way of knowing what Hodgson's beer looked like. Dr John Harrison, scientist and brewing historian, whose Durden Park Beer Circle in Maidenhead, Berkshire, recreates old beer style, brewed a beer as close as he could to Hodgson's recipe for a seminar on IPA held in London in 1994. He used pale malt only, with no brewing sugars, but he admits the beer could be no more than "an educated guess".

Changes in malting techniques in the late 18th century could have enabled Hodgson to brew a genuinely pale beer. Pale malt was a constituent element of the first "entire butt" or porter beers brewed almost a century earlier. But it was an expensive ingredient, made in country areas, with coal instead of the wood normally used to make brown malt. Coal not only gave off noxious gases that caused dense fogs in urban areas but also tainted malt with unpleasant flavours. Indirect rather than direct heat had to be used in coal-fired kilns that dried and cured malt. Once coke – coal without the gases – was developed, it became possible to make pale malt on a mass commercial basis. It was taken up with enthusiasm by brewers: pale malt, only lightly kilned, contained more enzymes than brown malt and therefore had more "diastatic power", the natural chemical ability to convert malt starches into fermentable sugar (maltose) during the mashing process.

The appeal of pale malt to brewers had little to do with the colour of the finished beer. Crucially, it meant they could cut their costs by using less pale malt than brown malt to achieve the desired level of alcohol. Even the porter and stout brewers moved from brown to pale malt in the early 19th century once

Daniel Wheeler had invented a roasting machine that enabled them to colour their beers with a dash of black or chocolate malts. It was the demand from India for a lighter and more sparkling and quenching ale that led Hodgson and his competitors to move to pale ale production. Dr Harrison is surely right in thinking that Hodgson's India Ale met that demand by being genuinely pale. One thing can be said without fear of contradiction: none of the early brewers of IPA could have used crystal malt, the stock-in-trade of modern producers of pale ale and bitter, as this type of stewed malt was not invented until late in the 19th century to give colour, body and flavour to a new type of draught ale known as "running beer". Far from being "copper coloured or reddish brown", the first IPAs brewed in Burton and later in Scotland were probably paler even than Hodgson's as the brewers used white malt, some of it imported from mainland Europe and the United States, that was similar to lager malt.

As the Burton brewers based their beers on Hodgson's, it is reasonable to suggest that the ale produced at Bow Bridge was around 1060 degrees original gravity or six per cent alcohol. As an experienced brewer, Hodgson knew that the best defences against spoilage on the arduous three-month voyage to India were alcohol and hops. As well as giving bitterness to beer, hops contain tannins and resins that fight bacteria, and the first IPAs had twice the hop rates of beers brewed for the domestic market. Additional hops may have been added to the finished casks as a further measure against infection along with priming sugar to keep the yeast active. The success of Hodgson's India Ale indicates that it arrived at its destination in sound and refreshing condition, though as the brewery was using London's soft well waters, best suited for mild and stout, the beer would have lacked the sparkle and flinty character of Burton ales. It was not colour but the water and the yeast strains developed in Burton that were to lead ultimately to the triumph of Burton-brewed pale ales.

Mark Hodgson, who succeeded his father, attacked the India market with even greater vigour. In 1750, some 1,480 barrels of beer left England for India. By 1775 the number had grown to 1,680. In 1800, 9,000 barrels were despatched, an increase that surpassed the entire amount of beer exported to India in the previous 100 years. Not all the beer came from Hodgson's, but the Bow Brewery was responsible for the bulk of it. Hodgson created a virtual monopoly in India but he was annoying powerful interests. The *Circular on Beer Trade to India* complained in 1829 of Hodgson's unethical methods. It claimed that when Hodgson heard that another brewer was shipping ale to India he would flood the market with large amounts of his own beer, driving down the selling price. The potential rival brewers suffered damaging losses as a result. Having seen off the competition, Hodgson then exploited scarcity by sending small supplies of ale the following year, forcing up prices in order to recoup his diminished profits from the previous year. Prices fluctuated from 20 rupees for a 54-gallon hogshead to 200 rupees.

Mark Hodgson made the mistake of annoying the powerful and influential East India Company. The company was a monopoly that controlled trade with the sub-continent. When Hodgson failed to pay his agents in India and even attempted to set up his own import business, the EIC decided to act. Over dinner in 1821, a director of the company named Marjoribanks told Samuel Allsopp, one of the leading Burton brewers, that lucrative pickings could be made from the India trade. According to Buchanan's book *Burton and Its Bitter Beer*, published in 1858, Marjoribanks told Allsopp that India offered "a trade that can never be lost: for the climate is too hot for brewing. We are now dependent upon Hodgson who has given offence to most of the merchants of India. But your Burton ale, so strong and sweet, will not suit our market." Marjoribanks' butler provided the diners with a bottle of Hodgson's ale. Allsopp, who had bemoaned the loss of his Baltic trade due to conflicts with France, hurried back to Burton with the sample of Hodgson's beer, which he presented to his head brewer, Job Goodhead. Goodhead said he could kiln his malt to produce a beer of that colour – further evidence that it really was pale – but he spat the beer out when he tasted it, affronted by its extreme hoppy bitterness. Hodgson's beer made a similarly poor impression on George's of Bristol, a major porter brewery that experimented with pale ale. In 1828 a senior partner at George's wrote to Willis & Earle in Calcutta suggesting it would not be difficult to improve on Hodgson's beer. "We neither like its thick and muddy appearance or rank bitter flavour," he added. Twenty months later, George's shipped 20 hogsheads to India and the same writer noted: "We made a slight alteration to the Ale by brewing it rather of a paler colour and more hop'd to make it as similar as possible to some samples of Allsopp's ale." For despite his initial revulsion, and under pressure from Allsopp, Job Goodhead had made a trial brew of a pale ale, using (according to legend) a tea pot as his mash tun. Allsopp soon had a supply of pale ale ready for the India trade. In a small town such as Burton, packed with breweries and where brewery workers mingled after hours in local taverns, news of the development spread rapidly. Bass and Thomas Salt, the other major Burton brewers, quickly experimented with their own ales for the India market. They were taking a considerable risk. They had to invest in large casks, hogsheads and 108-gallon butts, and, unlike Hodgson, had to pay transport costs to get the beer to London or Liverpool by canal before meeting the additional costs of the passage to India. And when the ales reached their destination they had to pass muster with tasters who could accept or reject a whole consignment. Allsopp heard to his horror that his first consignment, while accepted by the tasters, earned only 20 rupees a hogshead while Hodgson's rated 25. The second and third consignments from Allsopp brought 40 rupees per hogshead and from that moment the Burton brewer never looked back. A letter from a J C Bailton had given Allsopp great heart: "With reference to the loss you have sustained in your first shipments, you must have been prepared for that, had you known the market as well as I do: Here almost everything is name, and Hodgson's has so long stood without a rival that it was a matter of astonishment how your ale could have stood the competition; but that it did is a fact, and I myself was present when a butt of yours fetched 136 rupees, and a butt of Hodgson's only 80 rupees at a public sale."

Within a decade, Allsopp and Bass accounted for more than half the beer shipped to Calcutta, almost twice as much as Hodgson. Throughout the 1830s, the two Burton breweries sent some 6,000 barrels a year of pale ale to India. Hodgson was eclipsed and went into decline. The company was put up for sale in 1885 and a report in the weekly edition of *The Times* in July of that year said it had been sold to Smith, Garrett & Co. The list of brewery contents indicates that Hodgson's, which had been rebuilt in 1821, had been far removed from the "unremarkable" status afforded it by Gourvish and Wilson. The company was described as having "very extensive brewery premises...most prominently situate close to Bow-bridge, at the corner of the High-street, and covering a large area with the suitable buildings thereon, large malt and hop stores, numerous beer stores, tun rooms, vat rooms, lofty brewhouse with chimney shafts, engine and boiler houses, good brewer's residence with laboratory adjoining, roomy stabling, offices, and large yard with entrance gates from the road." The fact that Hodgson's site included a laboratory suggests it was a technically advanced brewery for its time. The company also owned three shops, a flour mills and 18 public houses in Bow, Poplar, Blackwall, Stratford, Barking, Mile End, Ilford, Walthamstow and Blackheath. Blackheath is on the south side of the Thames and a considerable distance from the site of the brewery, which lends credence to the belief that Hodgson's Kingston Brewery in Surrey may have had a family connection with the Bow enterprise. Certainly Hodgson's fame had not been confined to London. In 1908, the *Derby Chronicle* said: "Although Burton's reputation for brewing beer extends back almost to the Anglo-Saxon period, its most famous product – bitter ale – was not brewed there until 1822. At that time Hodgson's India pale ale, alluded to so appreciatively by Thackeray, which was brewed at Bromley-by-Bow, Middlesex, reigned supreme among light beers, being consumed not only in India, but, after a journey there and back to improve it, in England." The suggestion that Hodgson's aged its beer by sending it to India and back, a six-month voyage in all, seems fanciful, though unsold beer may have been returned to England and sold in Hodgson's pubs. Clearly, some of Hodgson's India Ale was available in London in order to inspire Thackeray, and to enable Samuel Allsopp's brewer to replicate it.

Far from disappearing in 1885, as most histories suggest, the Bow Brewery flourished under Smith, Garrett until 1927 when it was taken over by the leading London brewer Taylor Walker, based nearby at the Barley Mow Brewery, Limehouse. By this time, the Bow Brewer owned a substantial estate of more than 100 pubs. Taylor Walker closed the brewery. The site was demolished in 1933 and was turned into local authority flats named Prioress House, owned by the London County Council (photographs on next page).

Above and below: Prioress House, formerly the site of the Bow Brewery, purchased by another London brewer Taylor Walker in 1927, and demolished in 1933.

Burton

brewing capital
of the world

The torch passed to Burton-on-Trent in the East Midlands. Long before it was technically possible to brew pale ale, Burton enjoyed a reputation for the quality of its beer, as a piece of 19th-century doggerel affirms:

Ne'er tell me of liquors from Spain or from France,
They may get in your heels and inspire you to dance.
But Ale of old Burton if mellow and right
Will get in your head and inspire you to fight.

In 1002 AD, Wulfric Spot, the Earl of Mercia, founded a monastery in Staffordshire, and the monks of Burton Abbey settled to their devotions and the brewing of ale. They found that the spring waters from the wells in the valley of the River Trent produced beer with a fine taste and excellent keeping qualities. Centuries later, when it was possible to analyse Burton's waters, they were found to contain high levels of salts, in particular calcium sulphate (gypsum) and magnesium (Epsom salts). The salts encouraged a powerful fermentation, drew the best from the hops, and gave the finished beer a tempting sparkle and refreshing quality. London water, in contrast, was soft, high in calcium carbonate, and better suited to brewing brown beers: the water in the capital drew out of the sweetness of the malt sugars. (Readers will notice that my co-author does not necessarily agree that Burton's water was crucial to the quality and character of Burton pale ales. As a non-brewing writer, I listen with respect to his views, as I do also to the views of Paul Bayley of Marston's, brewer of the classic Burton pale ale, Pedigree.)

By 1600 Burton had 46 licensed victuallers who produced ales for a population of just 1,500. Burton ales began to gain a reputation outside the immediate area of their production, which was unusual at a time of rudimentary, slow transport. The beers reached London and became a cult drink in the Peacock in Gray's Inn Lane and the Dagger Inn in Holborn. By the early

18th century there were references in London journals to "Hull ale" but this was almost certainly beer from Burton that had reached the east coast port by way of the Trent and was then taken on to London by sea-going ships. In 1712, 638 barrels of Burton beer passed through Hull en route for London, and Joseph Addison, the celebrated journalist and playwright, noted in the *Spectator*, "We concluded our walk with a glass of Burton ale." The same paper reported that Burton beer was in great demand in the Vauxhall Pleasure Gardens. The Trent Navigation Act of 1699 had made the river navigable from Burton to Shardlow, and by 1712 it had been extended to Gainsborough and Hull. The Burton brewers sold their ales, brown, sweet and well-hopped, all over central and northern England. They were also exporting them to the Baltic ports.

Tsar Peter the Great of Russia and the Empress Catherine enjoyed the ales from far-away Burton-on-Trent. But 18th-century technology proved a bar to expanding exports. Benjamin Wilson, who founded the brewery that was to become Samuel Allsopp's, complained in a letter in 1791 to a customer in Elbing: "From the unusual impatience of the Shipowners and Masters to depart so early in the Spring, I ought to begin to brew before the Winter sets in; but let me tell them and all whom it may concern that it would be very dangerous to the preservation of the ale, which is a material object both for me and my friends to consider. I commonly begin to brew in the beginning of November, and am not willing, notwithstanding the importunity of the shipowners, to open my winter business sooner." Brewing in Burton as the century drew to its close was still a seasonal affair. Wilson complained that even a mild winter could force him to suspend brewing as he could not control his mashing and fermenting temperatures. And brewing methods were still archaic. In a letter to Joseph Brooks in London, Wilson explained: "Every part of the business is done by hand-pail, from drawing of the mash to filling the casks for exportation. It occurs to me that this quantity of business could be done with the aid of machinery to some great expense, and with equal certainty of purpose." Country brewing lagged behind London and other large cities, but Wilson, for one, was critically aware of the need to modernise.

He was also frustrated by his inability to produce an ale of standard colour and strength. In a further letter from 1791, in response to customers in the Baltic, he admitted: "I have committed one fault in the brewing of my ale last winter, and that is, in making it too strong – if I had made it weaker it certainly would have been lighter coloured and would have pleased better at first sight; but it is certainly better for the interest of the adventure to possess strength sufficient for its certain conservation, than to be otherwise and in danger of turning sour." This is a highly significant letter. Customers in the Baltic were clearly demanding a more refreshing beer. Wilson was anxious to please but at that stage could not meet the demand for a beer lighter in alcohol if not in colour. As an experienced brewer, he was aware that beer needed strength to survive long sea voyages. It was not just the journey that inhibited trade between Burton and the Baltic, a trade that at its peak accounted for 70 per cent of the brewers' production. Anglo-Russian trade declined as relations between the two countries soured. In 1783 tariffs on British goods imported through St Petersburg increased by 300 per cent. Trade ceased altogether when Russia placed an embargo on all British ships and merchandise. The Burton brewers turned their attentions to Prussia and Poland, and for a while business was brisk. William Bass, who sold his transport business in 1777 to a man named Pickford (whose business also flourished) to concentrate on brewing, had by the turn of the century nine agents in St Petersburg, 11 in Riga, 25 in Danzig, one in Elsinore, and four each in Bremen, Hamburg and Hanover.

The entire Baltic trade collapsed with the wars with France that lasted intermittently from 1799 to the defeat of Bonaparte at the Battle of Waterloo in 1815. As Bonaparte's armies rampaged across Europe they closed port after port to the British. Ships laden with Burton ale could make the increasingly hazardous sea crossings only if they were guarded by the Royal Navy, and the British Admiralty had better uses for its men o'war. The effect in Burton was catastrophic. Between 1780 and the mid-1820s, the number of breweries in the town fell from 13 to five. The bigger brewers – Wilson (in partnership with his nephew Samuel Allsopp), William Bass, Thomas Salt and William Worthington – desperately searched for new markets. They turned to the colonies for survival.

Britain first colonised India in 1772 and brewers hurried to supply beer first to the soldiers' garrisons and then the growing number of British civilians. But brown ales and porters were not the best thirst-quenchers in that torrid climate, and they tended to arrive sour and flat after a sea journey that lasted between three and five months. A brilliant piece of research by Thom Tomlinson, brewer of the previously mentioned Renegade Red IPA, working with the Climate Diagnostic Center in Boulder, Colorado, tracked the temperature fluctuations of a shipload of ale on a voyage between Britain and India in the mid to late

1800s. The research appeared in the March/April 1994 issue of the journal *Brewing Techniques*, published in Eugene, Oregon. The ships left between late November and early February, arriving in India between March and May. The winter departures were timed to make sure the ships reached the Indian Ocean before the monsoon season set in. Heading south from London, the ships crossed the equator, cruised south along the coast of Africa, rounded the Cape of Good Hope, and then crossed the Indian Ocean to Bombay, Calcutta and other ports of call.

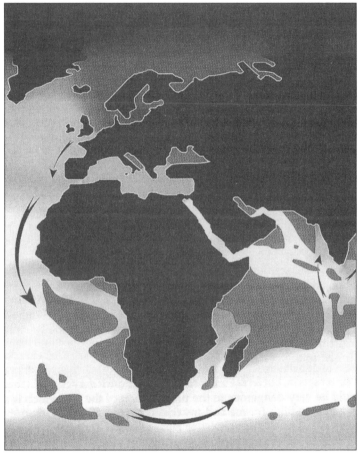

Map showing the temperature changes encountered by India Pale Ale in the hold, during a voyage to India.

"Even though the hogsheads of ale were stored in the lowest level of the ship's hull – the coolest place in the ship – the temperature fluctuations were tremendous," Tomlinson said. The research showed that for the first few weeks of the voyage, water temperatures were approximately 52 degrees F/11 degrees C. As the ships entered equatorial regions, temperatures climbed to 81 degrees F/25 degrees C. As they rounded the Cape, temperatures dropped to between 65-69 degrees F/17-19 degrees C. On the final leg of the voyage, nearing the coast of India, temperatures would reach 83-86 degrees F/26-28 degrees C. As Thom Tomlinson observed: "Combine the temperature fluctuations with the normal rocking motions of such a journey and the rough waters off southern Africa and you have one hellish trip for an ale."

The key to the success of Burton-brewed ales lies in the yeast created by the union system of fermentation and the spring waters of the Trent Valley. Paul Bayley, head brewer at Marston, Thompson & Evershed, the last Burton brewer to use the union method, describes the yeast strain as "greedy". It attacks the sugar in the wort ferociously, producing dry, "fully-attenuated" beers in which most of the sugars turn to alcohol. The use in the copper of substantial amounts of brewing sugar, which, unlike maltose, is almost totally fermentable, adds to the dryness and high alcohol of the finished beer. The beer is extremely stable but in cask it needs far longer to condition than non union-brewed beers. It survived the journey to India better than most beers and, according to Bayley, the active yeast in the casks fought bacteria. Burton water or "brewing liquor" played an equally important role in the flavour and keeping qualities of pale ale. According to Bayley, "Calcium reduces sugar and helps produce more alcohol. It keeps the yeast active, reduces haze, decreases beer colour and improves hop utilisation. The result is a more bitter beer. Magnesium acts in a similar fashion and sulphate gives a drier flavour and enhances bitterness."

Thom Tomlinson agrees with this assessment of Burton water. "The secret to the Burton brewers' success came from the water," he says, "an ingredient often downplayed in beer recipe formulation. The sulphates of the Trent basin helped the Burton beers achieve their clarity and bitterness, and allowed the Burton brewers to far exceed Hodgson's India Pale Ale in clarity, hopping rate, and marketability. The high sulphate content allowed brewers to use hopping rates well beyond that compatible with the carbonate water of London. Sulphates actually change the mouthfeel and perception of bitterness. High sulphate content results in a sharp, clean bitterness, unlike the harsh, clinging bitterness of highly-hopped beers brewed with water high in carbonates."

Few records survive from the 19th century, but Bass archivists claim that export ales brewed until the 1970s were based on recipes dating back to the 1850s. If true, this means a Bass pale ale for India would have had an original gravity of around 1060 degrees (approximately six per cent alcohol). This is not exceptionally strong for the time (stout porters were between seven and eight per cent) but assuming the casks were primed with sugar and vigorous second fermentation took place, the final alcohol content could have been higher. The ales were heavily hopped in the copper at a rate of between three and four pounds per barrel. Dry hops were added in cask at around six ounces per barrel. The units of bitterness, had they been capable of measurement in the 1850s, would have reached seventy or eighty, almost twice that of a modern bitter, but the bitterness would have softened during the sea voyage. Bass used Fuggles and Goldings from Kent and Worcestershire, varieties still in widespread use today, though modern varieties are considerably higher in the alpha acids that add bitterness to beer. Many British brewers used both Californian and German hops, which accounted for 50 per cent of the hop content of their beers. They also used imported barleys from the United States and mainland Europe. The relative cheapness of sea-borne imports allowed brewers to blend a wide variety of malt and hops, balancing out imperfections in any one particular batch.

Brewers abandoned the vatting of beers as a result of the success of India Pale Ale. Two American writers, Wahl and Henius, said in a book published in Chicago in 1908 that the vatting of pale ales went out of vogue with the triumph of the Burton brewers. Vatting had been the hallmark of strong stock ales made by country brewers, as well as porters blended with vatted "stale" ales that were attacked in their unlined wooden tuns by lactobacillus and such wild yeast strains as Brettanomyces. IPAs were brewed with long sea journeys in mind and vatting before racking into casks was unnecessary. Unlike vatted beers, which were not fully attenuated to leave some residual sweetness, IPAs were fully brewed out. When the giant hogsheads arrived at the docks in London or Liverpool, the bungs were removed and the natural carbon dioxide vented off, a precautionary measure to prevent the casks exploding in the holds of the ships, which would have been bad for the beer and possibly disastrous for the ships. The casks were then resealed and there was sufficient sugar (priming sugar may have been added at the docks) to encourage a slow second fermentation during the voyage to ensure the beer arrived in sparkling condition. The high levels of alcohol and hops were enough to ward off infection from bugs and wild yeasts.

Allsopp and Bass in Burton as well as the leading Scottish brewers who, as we shall see, moved enthusiastically to making their own versions of IPA, exported beer not only to India but also to Australasia, South America and the Caribbean. Some of it went in bottle as well as cask and this was increasingly the case as the century progressed. The Scots were pioneers in bottling beer. When Alfred Barnard, the noted Victorian writer on British and Irish breweries, visited James Aitken's brewery in Falkirk, he was astonished by the size of the bottling operation. He attributed the company's success in Australia and other colonies "not only to the quality of their beer, but to the cleanly, perfect, and careful nature of their bottling." Beer that was sent in casks was bottled on arrival. The yeast sediment continued to improve the beer in bottle. The bottles were stored in cool places, such as cellars in private homes or in the clubs of officers, gentlemen and "other ranks". In spite of the fact that British colonists were desperate for fresh consignments of India Ale, it is not clear if the beer was ready to drink on arrival. In 1858, an agent in Calcutta complained to the Edinburgh brewer William Younger: "Your beer is well known for its body. This is an obstacle to its becoming a favourite brand; it takes so long to ripen. The few casks of your last lot were fully 18 months before sufficiently ripe to drink". If this were a widespread problem, it would account for the rapid decline of IPA when confronted by star-bright, filtered lager beers ready for consumption on arrival at their destinations.

The India trade attracted brewers outside Burton. By 1833 Allsopp's and Bass's beers were joined at the docks by Barclay Perkins and Charrington from London and Tennent from Glasgow. In 1840 some 20,000 barrels of ale were exported to India, and the business rose to a peak of 217,000 barrels in 1870. By 1860 production of pale ale was the "first consideration" at Allsopps. Simonds of Reading began to brew "a novel kind of beer, pale ale, for export" in 1834. Simonds used its contacts with the British Army based at Aldershot to export beer to Cyprus, Egypt, Gibraltar, India and South Africa. Younger of Edinburgh had supplied bottled beer in 1865 to British troops fighting at Alma, Balaclava and Inkermann during the Crimean War. New markets opened up. The gold rush in Australia in the 1850s sent 400,000 British emigrants in search of wealth. The British brewers hurried to refresh them, if a minimum 68-day voyage by the fastest clipper could be described as hurrying.

From Australia it was a shorter journey to New Zealand. British beer was acclaimed there. In July 1857 Younger received an urgent appeal from its New Zealand agent: "We want show cards. Quality of ale approved of. Keep us supplied and we will do good business. We have the only underground cellar in Wellington, which is excellently adapted for malt liquors. Nelson Goldfields going ahead and only requires a spring to induce thousands to try their luck at them." In August 1858 the same agent wrote: "Your ale much liked and well-suited to our climate."

But not for long. In 1885 two Germans founded the Gambrinus Brewery in Melbourne. They were followed by the Foster brothers from the United States who started a second brewery dedicated to cold-fermented beers in the city. Castlemaine started to brew in Brisbane in 1889. In 1900 a Swiss brewer named Conrad Breutsch was invited to New Zealand specifically to brew lager beer. Ironically, he brewed at the Captain Cook Brewery in Auckland, named in honour of the Yorkshire sea captain who brewed a rough ale in New Zealand to cure his crew of scurvy. British brewers enjoyed similar success in the United States until the second wave of immigrants from central Europe brought with them the skill to brew cold-fermented lager beers. Records show that British brewers sent shipments of beer to America and the Caribbean in 1695. Samuel Whitbread was exporting beer to New York City by 1746, just four years after he had opened his brewery in London's Barbican. Bristol, with its strong sea links with North America, was also exporting beer by the mid-18th century. William Younger enjoyed such excellent sales for its Scotch Ale and India Ale that it employed its own agent in New York. But he could not prevent American brewers in the city passing off their own products, and he was forced to place the following advertisement in the press:

"Having the direct agency for the sale of William Younger and Co's Ales, Edinburgh, Scotland, I would caution the purchasers of Scotch Ale against the many spurious imitations sold, and in many instance bottled, in this city. To escape prosecution for forgery, they have slightly changed the spelling thus – 'Yonkers' – retaining the same style of bottles and colour, and otherwise a facsimile of the genuine label." Yonkers is a town close to New York City. The assiduous agent expressed his "acute disappointment" during the hot summer of 1856 that a consignment of Younger's India Ale had not arrived. He ordered 300 casks "without fail" by October and a further 300 by December. When 100 casks of Younger's ale were put on sale in

Boston they sold so fast that the importer told Edinburgh, "we could have sold readily 500 casks of your ale." A batch of beer sent to New Orleans was advertised in the press: "Expected per ship Oroondates from Liverpool, 336 casks Pale Ale, pints and quarts, 172 casks Strong Ale, pints and quarts, Wm Younger and company, Edinburgh, and for sale by Brulatour & Company, Sole Agents, Old Levee Street." An agent in Baltimore complained to Younger that he had ordered India Pale Ale but had been sent porter instead, an indication that American tastes were moving away from dark, heavy beer. Bass's Ale – the company never used the term IPA – was listed on the menu of the dining cars of the Union Pacific transcontinental railroad, and Allsopp's pale ale won prizes in the Centennial Brewers' Exhibition in Philadelphia in 1876.

The success enjoyed by British IPAs contained the seeds of its own downfall. Gabriel Sedlmayr the Younger, from the Spaten Brewery in Munich, and his colleague Anton Dreher from Vienna, the most important innovators where cold-fermented lager beer is concerned, embarked on a six-year grand tour of all the leading brewing nations to hone their skills. The technical and scientific advances in Britain left a deep impression. Bass presented Sedlmayr with a saccharometer so he could measure the fermentable sugars in wort. In spite of the generosity of their hosts, the visiting brewers engaged in an early form of industrial espionage. They used thermometers to secretly measure temperatures. They had hollowed-out walking sticks with hidden valves in which they kept samples of beer and wort for later analysis. They wrote home saying that even though they had been warmly welcomed in one brewery "we still stole as much as we could". "It always surprises me that we can get away with these thefts without being beaten up," Sedlmayr added. The young brewers were impressed in particular by new methods of kilning grain in Britain to produce pale malt. Sedlmayr took over the Spaten Brewery in 1836 following the death of his father. He embraced steam power and, later, refrigeration, but he continued to make brown beers, albeit by cold fermentation, as a result of a high tax on coal and the Bavarian preference for dark or "dunkel" beer. Dreher also embraced cold fermentation but used his British experience to produce an amber beer dubbed "Vienna Red", the first relatively pale beer seen in Europe.

The major breakthrough came in Bohemia in 1842 when the new Burghers' Brewery launched a golden lager. The brewer was a young Bavarian named Joseph Groll who was experienced in the new method of cold fermentation. The story still adhered to in Pilsen is that the golden lager was a "mistake" as a result of the wrong type of malt being delivered to Groll. It is far more likely that Groll set out to make a beer as distinctive as possible from Bavarian brown lager. He was aided by the character of the water in Pilsen, Moravian malt that was low in nitrogen, high levels of local Zatec [Saaz] hops, and by the knowledge picked up in Britain by Martin Stelzer, the architect of the Burghers' Brewery, better known today as Pilsner Urquell. Stelzer, following in the footsteps of Sedlmayr and Dreher, toured major brewing nations, including Britain, to help him with his designs for a modern brewery in Pilsen. Frustratingly, the Brewing Museum in Pilsen has no records to prove or disprove the possibility that Stelzer recommended that the Burghers' Brewery should buy a British coke-fired kiln to cure its malt, a sure way of producing the colour of grain that enabled Groll to fashion his golden lager.

The impact of Pilsner beer was immediate and on a world scale. Other breweries rushed to emulate the pale, refreshing beer from Bohemia. As Germany and the United States hurried to catch up with the international manufacturing dominance of Britain, they introduced their own beer styles into countries formerly under the sway of British ales. The Japanese, who had never brewed beer, were encouraged to do so by an American trade mission in 1853 that was accompanied by a contingent of the US Navy, a novel reason for sending a gunboat. Under the onslaught of lager beer, British exports of pale ale were falling fast by the 1880s. *The Brewers' Journal* in August 1882 castigated the big brewers – Bass, Allsopp, Barclay Perkins and Guinness – for not seizing the opportunity to dominate the world export market in beer. "Bottled Bass," the journal proclaimed, "has been found in every country where Englishmen had yet put foot" but now Bass and the others had become complacent and were failing to match the zeal of the Germans, who were building breweries in their African colonies and even in China. A colonial critic of the British brewers complained their beers had "too much alcohol, too much sediment, too much hops and too little gas". The brewers were not prepared to change their methods. They had invested massively in new plant and were not willing to switch to even more capital-intensive lager plant. And they had found a captive market for pale ale on their doorstep.

Bass coopers in the 19th century.

In 1827 a ship carrying some 300 hogsheads of India Pale Ale was wrecked in the Irish Sea. Both Allsopp and Bass have claimed the consignment was theirs. A Bass guidebook published in 1902 said, "A quantity saved was sold in Liverpool on behalf of the Underwriters. The quality was so much appreciated that the fame of the new 'India Beer' spread in a remarkably rapid manner throughout Great Britain." That is an exaggeration. Sales of "India Beer" did not grow until 1839 as a result of railway mania. The opening of the Birmingham to Derby railway gave the Burton brewers access to England's second city, and from there into the burgeoning national rail network. When St Pancras Station was built in London, its cellars were designed specifically to house hogsheads of Bass beer. During the 1840s, the output of Burton's breweries increased from 70,000 to 300,000 barrels a year. Allsopp and Bass were responsible for 70 per cent of the output. Between 1850 and 1880 Burton brewing trebled in size every 10 years. Bass forged ahead of its main rival, Allsopp. By 1874 Bass, with an annual output of 900,000 barrels, had become the biggest brewing company in the world. By the turn of the century it had a yearly production of one and half million barrels and a workforce of 2,760.

The London brewers faced a quandary. They could not "do a Hodgson" and brew an inferior India Ale now that Burton pale ales were widely available. With the abolition of the tax on glass in 1845 and the replacement of pewter tankards by glass containers, the demand for pale ale soared. Lacking the ability to treat the soft London waters to replicate the hard ones of Burton, the London brewers opened second plants in the East Midlands town to take advantage of the salt-rich spring waters. Middleton, Nunneley and the substantial Romford brewery of Ind Coope opened breweries in Burton in the 1840s and 1850s. The increasing success and prosperity of their Burton competitors forced Charrington, Mann Crossman & Paulin, and Truman to also open shop in Burton. Provincial brewers followed. Boddingtons of Manchester, A B Walker and Peter Walker from Warrington, and Everards of Leicester built plants in what was now the undisputed capital of British brewing. With the exception of Ind Coope, which eventually merged with Allsopps in 1934, the incomers did not enjoy great success in Burton. Mann Crossman & Paulin had a fine reputation for its London mild ale but its Burton pale ale was not similarly regarded. Truman was considered to brew a good version of IPA but it did not enjoy the high reputation of Allsopp and Bass. By the end of the century most of the incomers had retreated back to London, Manchester and Warrington, by which time their scientists had discovered how to "Burtonise" their brewing liquors by adding gypsum and magnesium salts.

Every brewer had to have an India Pale Ale in his portfolio. As early as 1855 the Stafford Brewery's price list included X Ale, XX Ale, XXX Ale, Stafford Imperial, AK Ale, IPA, Porter, Stout, Single Stout and Double Stout. Pale ale was not cheap. It cost around seven to eight pence a quart against four or five pence for mild or porter. Richard Wilson, in *The British Brewing Industry 1830-1980*, argues that "Quality and cost...made it [Burton pale ale] a status drink for the expanding lower middle class of clerks and shopkeepers, the armies of rail travellers, and those 'aristocrats of labour' [highly skilled workers] whose standard of living rose appreciably after 1850...Making a good Burton-type ale was the sine qua non for that generation of brewers who reaped the rewards of the great increase in consumption in the 1860s and 1870s." When the duty on glass was lifted, pale ale looked tempting to drink, Wilson adds. "It became the high-fashion beer of the railway age." The pale ale brewers exploited the switch to glass in a second way: their beers were available in bottle for home consumption. This gave them snob value. The new and growing lower middle classes, conscious of their status, could now drink beer in the comfort of their homes, freed from the awful necessity of visiting the public houses of the working class.

The large brewers, enormously successful and wealthy – in Samuel Johnson's epic phrase, "rich beyond the dreams of avarice" – were keen to maximise profits by brewing beer in the most efficient manner possible. Louis Pasteur's work *Études sur la Bière*, and the later work of Emil Christian Hansen in the Carlsberg Laboratory in Copenhagen, had a profound effect. It became possible to isolate pure strains of yeast, prevent infection and spoiled beer, and to brew in the summer months. In 1895 the *Journal of the Institute of Brewing* noted caustically that the time had gone when a brewery could be regarded as "the last resource for a young man when, having failed for the Army, the church, or one of the learned professions, his premium is paid and he is shipped off to some pupil-taking brewery with the idea that 'at least we make a brewer of him.'" The journal stressed that the modern brewer should be "essentially a chemist, as brewing is practically the conversion of certain substances into certain chemically different substances by what is more or less a chemical process". Even before Pasteur published his findings in 1876, Allsopp had taken on a brilliant young German chemist, Dr Henry Böttinger of Wurtenburg, as the company's scientific adviser. Bass appointed John Matthews as its "chemist and principal brewer" and the legendary Cornelius O'Sullivan joined him in 1865. O'Sullivan's outstanding work won him many awards and in 1885 he was appointed a Fellow of the Royal Society. It was his pioneering research that enabled brewers to move from seasonal to all-year-round production. Dr Horace Tabberer Brown at Worthington carried out research into barley germination, yeast nutrition and microbiology that was to prove of far-reaching importance. He, too, became a member of the Royal Society. His half-brother, Dr Adrian Brown, worked for Thomas Salt until 1900, when he left to establish the British School of Malting and Brewing at the University of Birmingham. The brewing scientists in Burton formed a circle with the tongue-in-cheek name of the Bacterium Club. They were paid handsomely and were given excellent premises and the most up-to-date equipment. O'Sullivan was paid £3,500 a year by Bass, an enormous salary for the time.

**Cornelius O'Sullivan was paid handsomely by Bass
for his chemist's skills.**

Their research played a key role as the nature of brewing changed in the late 19th century. India Pale Ale had been a means to an end to carve out a lucrative export market to replace the trade lost to the Baltic States. Those ales, by necessity, had not only been high in alcohol but also massively hopped. By the 1880s, drinkers in Britain, the middle class consumers of pale ale in particular, were demanding less potent and less bitter beers. Critics of IPA complained of the style's "narcotic" effects, causing sleepiness as well as drunkenness. The brewers responded, but the response was due less to consumer preference than to a crisis in the industry that threatened their profitability. The 1830 Beer Act had allowed anyone to open a beer shop for an annual licence fee of two guineas. The number of licensed premises in the country virtually doubled as a result (in the late 19th century there were 100,000 licensed premises in Britain compared to 60,000 today). Many of the beer shops were badly run and their beer was poor. The commercial brewers bought up many of the beer shops, and also began to supply the growing number of "free trade" pubs. In order effectively to tie

30

these free trade pubs to one supplier's products, the brewers had to offer attractive loans and discounts. The property scramble sent prices soaring while loans and discounts were running at such high a level that several large breweries faced ruin. In 1896 Barclay Perkins was owed two million pounds by bankrupt publicans. Allsopp was so badly affected that it went into receivership and had to be financially restructured. By the turn of the century, brewers had become substantial owners of tied pub estates that had been built at astonishing cost. As many of the breweries were now public companies and faced angry shareholders, they had to take drastic action to restore their fortunes. They were no longer prepared to lock up capital in vats and casks, waiting months and even years for the money to come in.

At the close of the 19th century, therefore, the brewers had largely abandoned vatted porters, stock ales and IPAs matured in cask for months to what were dubbed "running ales". E R Moritz, consulting chemist to the Country Brewers' Society, wrote in the *Brewers' Almanack* of 1895: "It is…essentially within the last 10 years that these lighter ales, both of pale and mild character, have come especially to the front. The public in this period has come to insist more and more strongly upon extreme freshness of palate with a degree of brilliancy and sparkle their fathers never dreamt of." In 1905, Julian Baker wrote in *The Brewing Industry*, "the light beers, of which increasing quantities are being brewed every year, are more or less the outcome of the demand of the middle classes for a palatable and easily consumable beverage. A good example of this type of beer is the so-called 'family ale', and the cheap kinds of bottled bitter beers and porters."

The new pale ales were the product of scientific research and practice. All brewers could now Burtonise their liquor. Treated with sulphates, brewing liquor contributed to better extraction of malt sugars, improved hop utilisation and cleaner fermentation. Malting had been greatly improved, and the move to pale malt meant that more sugary extract could be produced from smaller amounts of grain. The scientific understanding of yeast was also a powerful impetus to producing running ales. Pure strains meant fermentation could be better controlled. Yeast packed down and cleared in cask within a few days, enabling beer to "drop bright" and be served within a day or two of arriving in the pub cellar. The use of stewed crystal malt, in which the starches are turned to non-fermentable dextrin, gave the new type of beer "body" or full flavour that masked its lack of true maturity. It was the copper colour of running beers – increasingly dubbed "bitter" by drinkers – that distinguished the style from IPA.

The terms IPA, pale and bitter are not interchangeable. Historically, IPA meant a "keeping beer" brewed to withstand long journeys and with bitterness levels that would have made them undrinkable save for the fact that the beers softened during sea voyages. Pale ale was a modified version of IPA brewed for the domestic market with a lower alcohol level and a considerable reduction in hop bitterness. Over time, pale ale came to mean a bottled beer while bitter indicated draught. While the term "bitter" was used as early as 1858, as in Buchanan's book *Burton and its Bitter Beer*, it did not come into vogue until the 20th century and the development of "running ales".

IPA had served its purpose. It had transformed brewing in Britain, and had even inspired the first brewers of commercial lager beers. British brewers continued to keep IPAs in their portfolios but in the 20th century they were minority brands, playing second fiddle to the pale ales and bitters they had spawned.

Export or die
the Scottish experience

India Pale Ale's success in England resonated in Scotland. In 1837, W H Roberts, in *The Scottish Ale Brewer and Practical Maltster*, wrote: "Up to about 1820 this trade [in IPA] was almost exclusively in the hands of Mr Hodgson. His beer was well-known in India, and highly appreciated." A Huguenot refugee named Robert Disher brewed the first pale ale in Edinburgh in 1821. He bought the Edinburgh and Leith Brewery in Edinburgh's Canongate and found, as did the brewers in Burton-on-Trent, that Edinburgh's water was ideally suited to brewing an India-type beer. It was high in calcium and sulphate, and bubbled to the surface through the Red Metals, the red sandstone and cement stone strata of the Charmed Circle, an underground trough of water-bearing strata that rings the centre of the city. Wells, rich in hard water, stretched from Holyrood in the east of the city through Canongate, Cowgate and the Grassmarket to Fountainbridge.

Edinburgh has been an important brewing centre since at least the 12th century, when monks brewed at Holyrood Abbey. By the time Robert Disher fashioned his India Ale in the 1820s, the Scottish capital had 25 breweries, some of them sizeable concerns. The predominant beer style was Scotch Ale, dark, strong and potent, and dubbed "Scottish Burgundies" by French aristocrats who settled in Edinburgh to escape the guillotine back home. While the great region that incorporated Edinburgh and Glasgow industrialised in step with England, the rest of Scotland, the Highlands in particular, remained poor and economically backward. North of the central belt there was little opportunity to sell beer. In *Highland Tours* written in 1804, James Hogg, the poet and novelist, recorded his experience at Rannoch Moor: "The day was very hot, and we arrived at the King's House, in the Black Mount, almost parched with thirst. 'Have you any porter?' said Mr L. on entering. 'Naneal,' said the wife. 'And ale?' said he – 'Oh! That's very good.' We were sorry to find she answered in Gaelic, and that she had neither the one nor the other. She had, however, plenty of tea, the only beverage in the Highlands that a stranger can partake freely." Scottish brewers, who were concentrated where the best grain for brewing grew, exported to England and further afield. France, as a result of the Auld Alliance, took substantial supplies of Scottish ale, as did the Low Countries and the Baltic States. By the close of the 18th century, small consignments were being despatched to expatriate Scots in the tobacco and sugar plantations in North America and the West Indies. Scotch Ale also found its way to the new markets of India and the Far East. With daunting wine-like strengths of around 1100 degrees original gravity (approximately 11 per cent alcohol in modern terms), the ales were well able to survive long sea journeys and arrive at their destinations in good condition.

Label from an Alloa India Pale Ale.

As overseas trade revived after the Napoleonic Wars, Scottish brewers found themselves facing a new challenge from Burton pale ales. Between 1830 and 1850, Edinburgh brewers moved swiftly to meet the challenge. They were blessed with natural water almost as hard as Burton's and the low ambient temperatures in Scotland kept fermentation temperatures low and enabled them to brew all year round. Famous names in Edinburgh brewing, including Drybrough, Campbell and Younger, moved to pale ale production. Alloa, equally blessed with hard, pure water, became another major brewing centre and was dubbed "the Burton of the North" by that hard-working scribe Alfred Barnard. It had eight breweries in the second half of the 19th century and George Younger's brewery was the third largest in Scotland. Ballinghall in Dundee also became a major producer of pale ale. Glasgow, with its soft water, was – like London – better suited to porter brewing and never became an important centre for pale ale. The new beer style offered considerable cost advantages over Scotch Ale and porter. Pale and amber malts were used more sparingly than dark malt while shorter fermentation and conditioning times brought a quicker turnover. As pale ales were lower in gravity than Scotch Ales, they attracted lower rates of duty. This was of particular importance from 1880 when William Gladstone's Budget levied duty on the original gravity of the wort in the mash tun instead of on raw ingredients.

Edinburgh India Pale Ale differed in several ways from the English versions. Brewing methods were different, while Scottish raw materials gave distinctive aromas and flavours to the beers. W H Roberts noted that in Scotland mashing took place at much higher temperatures than in England while fermentation was a long, slow process at a low temperature, similar to primary fermentation in lager brewing. Good quality malting barley was imported from England and overseas, but if such ancient Scottish varieties as Bere and Bigg, followed by more modern strains such as Annat, Scotch Chevalier and Scotch Common, were used then the finished ales had palates and characters quite different from Burton pale ales. The cold climate prevented hops from being grown in Scotland. As a result of the cost of importing hops from England, the hop rates of Scottish pale ales were comparatively low. T Thomson, in *Brewing & Distilling*, 1842, quotes a pound of hops per bushel of malt for Edinburgh "keeping ales", two-thirds the rate of Burton ales. When the hops were added to the copper, the boiling time was long by English standards. This led to some caramelisation of the brewing sugars. With the addition of amber malt, the finished beer was darker (approximately 30-40 on the EBC colour range), sweeter and stronger than the Burton equivalent. It was called "pale" in the sense that it was paler that Scotch Ales.

By 1890 around a third of exported British beer came from Scotland. Edinburgh, which by then had some 40 breweries, enjoyed the lion's share of the trade. The biggest breweries, such as McEwan and Younger, both of which became public companies in the brewery boom of the late 19th century, embraced the latest technologies. They introduced steam, gas and electric power, installed laboratories, and employed trained brewers and chemists. Refrigeration cut down on cooling and conditioning times, allowing even quicker turnover. The enhanced profit margins on pale ale were not lost on the Edinburgh brewers. They promoted their products with vigour, using advertising campaigns and allusions to imperial grandeur that were appreciated by jingoistic drinkers in the late Victorian period.

Domestic versions of beers variously dubbed Imperial, India or Export Ale grew in popularity, though they were usually brewed to lower strengths. The development of the railway enabled the brewers to move their beer around the country more easily. Pale ale quickly became the dominant beer style in Scotland and was also in great demand in Newcastle and North-east England. Employers welcomed the new style of beer. The capital investment involved in industrialising Central Scotland and North-east England demanded new levels of discipline from the workforce, and pale ale was seen as an antidote to whisky and stronger Scotch Ales.

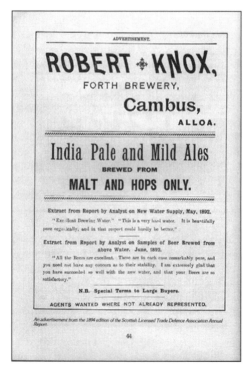

Advertisement for ales from the Forth Brewery.

36

Bottled beer met the needs of a country where many people still lived in rural isolation and there were fewer towns and cities than in densely populated England. When excise duty on glass was lifted in 1845 and mechanised bottle manufacture replaced hand-blowing, Scottish brewers started to bottle their products with alacrity. As in England, pale ale was best suited to clear glass bottles as its clarity and natural sparkle appealed to the drinker's eye. The trend towards IPA was now irreversible. When Alfred Barnard visited Younger's brewing sites in Edinburgh in the late 1880s he found that the entire production of the Holyrood brewery was given over to pale ale. "Their principal manufacture," he wrote, "is India Pale Ale, which is well known and appreciated in all parts of Britain as well as in foreign countries." By 1900 Scotland was exporting 123,000 barrels of beer annually, much of it in the form of pale ale from Edinburgh, which accounted for 80 per cent of all Scotland's beer production. The Scottish capital, said Barnard, was Burton and London rolled into one. Brewers moved there to take advantage of the water. Paterson and Maclachlan of Glasgow, Murray from the Borders and Deuchar from Tyneside switched their operations to Edinburgh to meet the insatiable demand for pale ale.

Scotland's reliance on export trade – between 1880 and the 1950s, the country provided around a quarter of all British beer exports – turned from an asset into a fetter. When Britain began to retreat from empire after World War Two, former colonies developed their own brewing industries and imposed high tariffs on imports. Exports of Scottish ales slumped alarmingly and the situation was made worse as British garrisons, for long important captive markets for Scottish beers, were dismantled. The collapse of the colonial trade followed the severe economic depression and chronic unemployment of the 1930s, a period of massive decline in brewing volumes. When the two modern giants of Scottish brewing, Tennent Caledonian (later a subsidiary of Bass) and Scottish & Newcastle, were formed in the 1960s they brought together no fewer than 15 leading Scottish breweries, including Tennent of Glasgow, William Younger and William McEwan of Edinburgh, and James Calder and George Younger of Alloa. Since the 1880s, Scottish brewers had experimented with lager and Tennent of Glasgow is credited with being the first brewer of the style in the British Isles. Lager appealed to many Scots on two grounds: its lightness of flavour, low bitterness and slight sweetness made it an ideal "chaser" for whisky, while many expatriate Scots acquired a taste for German, Australian and American lagers when they worked overseas.

Tennent Caledonian and S&N acted like all monopolies or duopolies: they concentrated on big volume brands with long shelf lives. Lager and keg [filtered and pasteurised] ales fitted the bill better than cask-conditioned pale ales that had to mature and "drop bright" in bars and required a modicum of skill from publicans. The problem of handling cask ale was exacerbated by the lack of a substantial tied trade in Scotland. Traditionally, brewers do not own bars or hotels, preferring to buy loyalty through loans and discounts. The fact that brewers have little control over the quality of the end product proved another nail in the coffin of cask-conditioned beer in Scotland until the arrival of CAMRA north of the border and then the boom in small craft breweries in the 1990s. S&N still brews considerable volumes of McEwan's Export for keg and can and represents one link with the hey-day of Scottish pale ale, though at a much-reduced strength. (Ironically, when the beer was bottle conditioned, a sample of the yeast was cultured at the Brewing Faculty at Leuven University in Belgium and used to launch the celebrated Belgian strong pale ale, Duvel.) The independent Caledonian Brewery in Edinburgh, which has no connection with Tennent Caledonian, has won many awards for its magnificent cask-conditioned Deuchar's IPA, though the genuine pallor of the beer gives it more of an English character than a true Scottish one.

Caledonian Brewery building, home of the re-created Deuchar's IPA.

Revival

nterest in India Pale Ale and pale ale grew in Britain in the 1990s as a result of a small seminar on the subject held in a south London pub that led on to a major conference, with brewers on both sides of the Atlantic producing interpretations of IPA for the occasion. Mark Dorber, manager of the White Horse, Parson's Green, sells Draught Bass and developed a fascination with Burton pale ales. In 1990, working with Dr Keith Thomas of the Brewers' Laboratory, Dorber organised a seminar at the pub attended by brewers from Bass, Burton Bridge and Marston's, experts on malt, hops and good cellar practice, and several leading beer writers. Dorber published the papers presented to the seminar and in 1993 approached Bass, owner of the pub, with the suggestion that it should brew an IPA for a planned festival of pale ales at the White Horse. Bass was enthusiastic and called in a retired brewer, Tom Dawson, for his advice. Dawson recalled brewing a beer called Bass Continental for the Belgian market from the 1950s to the 1970s. The beer was based on recipes for Bass pale ales brewed in the 1850s and therefore represented an unbroken line with the original IPAs, which were all fermented from worts with original gravities in the region of 1063 degrees. He consulted old brewing ledgers going back to the 1880s and drew up a recipe for the White Horse India Pale Ale. On Saturday 19 June 1993 a team of young brewers under Tom Dawson's guidance assembled at Burton-on-Trent to brew the beer, with the support of Mark Dorber and cellar staff from the White Horse.

The atmosphere, according to Dorber, was electric as they attempted to brew a taste of history. Brewing took place in the Bass Museum housed in the old engine shed at Burton. It includes a 1920s five-barrel pilot plant built for the Mitchells and Butlers Cape Hill Brewery in Birmingham in the 1920s to make experimental brews. It was moved to the museum in the late 1970s and has successfully recreated several old Bass beers, including the renowned No 1 barley wine. Two brews were necessary to meet the White Horse's demand for six hogsheads or 324 gallons. Brewing began at 6am and, working in two shifts, production of the beer took 29 hours. Tom Dawson's recipe was as follows:

**Mark Dorber samples an IPA
in the cellar at the White Horse.**

Original Gravity: 1063 degrees
Malt: 90 per cent of extract
Sugar: 10 per cent of extract
Hop rate: 3.6 lb per barrel (1.5g/brl) of Fuggles [actually
             Progress: see notes below]
             Two thirds at charge, one-third late (40 minutes
             before cast)
             6 ozs/brl dry hops [Goldings]
Boil time: three hours
Mash initial heat: 150 degrees F (66C)
Sparge heat: 162 degrees F (72C)
Pitching heat: 56 degrees F (13C)
Pitching rate: 2.8 lb/brl (1.1 kgs/brl) as barm

Mark Dorber's notes on materials and method used were:

Malt: 90 per cent Halycon pale malt and 10 per cent sugar.
Hops: Progress whole hops in copper at the very high rate of 3.5
lb per barrel – this is a "Fuggles-type" hop with low to medium
bittering qualities but whose alpha acid yield at 7 per cent was
40 per cent higher than the assumption underpinning Tom's IPA
recipe, resulting in a beer with significantly greater bitterness
than planned. Dry hopped with East Kent Goldings at the rate
of 6 oz per barrel.
Wort from copper was run over a bed of Progress in the

40

collecting vessel prior to cooling to strain and further clarify the wort and give a little extra hop aroma.

Yeast: yeast pitched was the two-strain Draught Bass yeast whose ancestry dates back to the Burton unions [Bass scrapped the unions in the 1980s]. It was a "second generation" yeast, i.e. cropped from the first brew produced with yeast propagated from an original slide. This yeast was thought likely to yield the best results in terms of its attenuative properties and its ability to undergo a long secondary fermentation in cask.

Water: water was de-ionised well water with a salt content adjusted to reflect high levels of gypsum – a critical element in the production of pale sparkling ales.

Will age beer in cask for five weeks before dispense on 31 July. Will continue to sell the IPA during August until it runs out.

Technical results:

Fermenting vessel 1:
Original Gravity 1064
Alcohol by Volume 6.8 per cent
Colour Units 21
Bitterness Units 88

Fermenting Vessel 2:
Original Gravity 1064
Alcohol by Volume 7.2 per cent
Colour Units 18
Bitterness Units 83

When the beer went on sale at the White Horse, I hurried to the pub and reported my findings in *What's Brewing*, newspaper of the Campaign for Real Ale. "The beer is burnished gold in colour. Placed next to a glass of modern Draught Bass and classic Pilsner Urquell lager beer, the White Horse IPA was midway between the two. The aroma was pungent and resiny. Hops dominated the palate and the long, intense bitter finish. 'It's like putting your head inside a hop pocket from the Kent fields,' Mark Dorber said. Malt and yeast also had their say in the aroma and palate of the beer. Ripe bananas, pear drop and apple esters began to make themselves felt as the beer warmed up. The fruitiness was most apparent when the beer was tasted in the pub cellar, straight from the cask. Dorber said a slightly higher fermenting temperature in the brewery than planned had helped create the fruity esters. He said the beer would remain in drinkable condition for some three months. Tom Dawson, with his long experience of Bass yeast, thinks it will survive for even longer. Both think the beer will become softer over time but will not lose the enormous hop character."

The renewed interest in the subject led to Dorber and the author, with the support of the British Guild of Beer Writers, organising a further seminar on the subject in the summer of 1994. We invited brewers in both Britain and the United States to participate, and to contribute beers for sampling. In preparation for the event, I asked Carlsberg-Tetley, the company that then owned the Ind Coope Brewery in Burton-on-Trent, if it would consider recreating an IPA, as Samuel Allsopp had brewed the first Burton pale ale on the site. Carlsberg-Tetley responded favourably and I went to the brewery to watch the beer being brewed. Ind Coope had a pilot plant known as the Samuel Allsopp Brewery. It was a miniature version of the group's brew-houses in Alloa, Scotland and Wrexham in Wales, built in the Netherlands and designed to produce lager beer. There was a certain historic irony in watching a Burton India Pale Ale being mashed in both a mash kettle and a lauter tun, for the system is the classic lager brewing one in which the wort is clarified not in the mash tun but in the lauter vessel. As a result of mergers and a turbulent financial history, the longest surviving recipes in the brewery date back only as far as 1935, one year after the merger of Ind Coope and Allsopp. Production director Peter Sunderland chose the recipe for an IPA that was brewed on 15 May 1935. It was a "parti-gyle" brew that produced a 1040 degrees bitter, a 1041 IPA and 1046 best bitter, the brew being treated with liquor after fermentation to produce beers of different gravities. The fact that the IPA had a lower gravity than the best bitter indicates how far the style had been Bowdlerised by the 1930s. The grist composition was fascinating. The brewery used pale and mild malts, probably Spratt Archer. The hops came from California (Biddell variety) and New Zealand (Buxton) as well as England. The English varieties were Hubble and Leake, both now extinct. Peter Sunderland said it was common in those days to use imported barleys from warmer climates, while California hops were free from European diseases and were high in alpha acids. (Hops are no longer grown in California: the industry now operates from the cooler climes of Oregon and Washington State.) As well as malt, three types of brewing sugar were used: Martineau's, Distiller's and Shardlow. With none of the ingredients available in 1994, Peter Sunderland and his team recreated the beer using modern varieties. Their task was made easier with the knowledge that the IPA was identical to a beer called Diamond that was brewed until 1960.

Sixty barrels of 1994 IPA were brewed from Halcyon pale malt, with 50 kilos of crystal malt and five kilos of chocolate malt, with 25 per cent brewing sugar. The hops were equal amounts of Fuggles and Goldings, and the finished beer was dry hopped in cask at the rate of four ounces per barrel. The beer was 4.2 per cent alcohol by volume, had 19 units of colour and 22 units of bitterness. The beer, despite the use of coloured malts, was similar in colour to the Bass IPA but, as the bitterness rating indicates, had a more gentle hoppiness. The Fuggles and Goldings nevertheless gave a fine peppery and citric fruit aroma, there was more tart fruit in the mouth, and the finish was quenching and finely balanced between malt and hops.

When the seminar assembled in the imposing surroundings of Whitbread's Porter Tun Room in the old Chiswell Street brewery in London, it attracted not only brewers, historians and beer writers but also the wine writers Oz Clarke, Andrew Barr and Andrew Jefford. Dr John Harrison of the Durden Park Beer Circle outlined the history of the style and reported that, in order to prove that IPAs could survive the journey to India and further afield, he had brewed a pale ale to a 19th-century recipe and kept it in his garage at a temperature of 80 degrees F/25 degrees C during the famous British hot summer of 1976. The beer was in good drinking condition the following Christmas. For the seminar he had brewed a beer that was as close as possible to what his research suggested Hodgson's India Ale would have been like. He used Thames Valley well water and 100 per cent pale malt, with no brewing sugars. The hops were East Kent Goldings with 5.5 per cent alpha acid, used at the rate of $2^1/_2$ ounces per gallon, and dry hopped at the rate of half an ounce per gallon. It was fermented from an original gravity of 1072 degrees using a yeast strain from Truman's. The beer was six weeks old at the seminar and had been fined three weeks earlier. It had a powerful resiny aroma of Goldings, was packed with tart fruit in the mouth, and the finish was exceptionally dry and bitter with a touch of astringency.

Paul Bayley of Marston's brought samples of an IPA that was 5.2 per cent alcohol and brewed from 100 per cent Pipkin pale malt. He used three hop varieties, Challenger, Fuggles and Goldings, and the beer was dry hopped at the rate of four ounces per barrel. The beer was well matured at eight weeks. It had a pungent sulphury nose – the famous "Burton snatch" – with undertones of grain and peppery hops. There was tart gooseberry fruit in the mouth and the finish was subtly fruity and hoppy.

Whitbread's Castle Eden Brewery in North-east England brewed an IPA with 5.5 per cent alcohol and 10 per cent torrefied wheat. Only Fuggles hops were used and the wort was late hopped in the copper for aroma. The colour, an appealing burnished gold, was 14 units, with 42 units of bitterness. The aroma had a ripe orange/citrus character with resiny hops. There were tart fruit and hops in the mouth, and the finish was a complex balance of quenching fruit and hops.

There was great interest in the Bass White Horse IPA, by then 11 months old. Mark Dorber said that to counter the pronounced banana ester on the beer, he had dry hopped the casks a second time in the cellar of the pub. The beer had become much softer over time. The fruitiness was almost Madeira-like, with a pungent apricot fruit on the nose, fruit, hops and nuts in the mouth, and a big bitter-sweet finish.

From the United States, Thom Tomlinson brought a sample of his Renegade Red, which had won a gold medal at the 1993 Great American Beer Festival. Tomlinson said he Burtonised his brewing liquor to enhance the fruitiness and bitterness of the beer. He used pale malt and 10 per cent crystal malt, and hopped the beer with two US varieties, Cascade (75 per cent) and Chinook, at the rate of two pounds per barrel. The beer was brewed from a gravity of 1064 degrees and had a literally stunning 90 units of bitterness. Bitter hops and tart fruit dominated the aroma and palate, and the finish was stunningly dry. Teri Fahrendorf of the Steelhead Brewery in Eugene, Oregon, brewed her Bombay Bomber from two-row pale malt and six-row Munich and Vienna coloured malts. It was 5.3 per cent alcohol by volume with 45 units of bitterness, She added gypsum to mountain water and hopped with Chinook and Mount Hood. The beer was dry hopped with Chinook, which gave a pungent gooseberry note to aroma and palate. With a lower bitterness level than Renegade Red's, the beer was a fine balance between malt and hops, it was refreshing in the mouth and dry in the finish.

Garrett Oliver's IPA from the Manhattan Brewery (brewer and beer have since crossed the bridge to brew at Brooklyn Brewery) had an original gravity of 1066 and was brewed from imported two-row East Anglian pale malt produced by Munton & Fison, with 25 per cent brewing sugar. It was dry hopped, primed with cane sugar and stored for three to four months. It reached 55 units of bitterness. The aroma was reminiscent of apricots and oranges, with great hop character and a big hoppy/bitter finish. It was both a magnificent beer and brewed with enormous dedication to style.

**Garrett Oliver brought an IPA
from the Manhattan Brewery.**

The seminar concluded with a call to British brewers to make more commercial versions of IPA available. Those present felt that any beer labelled IPA, if it is true to style, should not be less than 5.5 per cent alcohol and 40 units of bitterness. Sadly, the enthusiasm of brewers and beer writers at the seminar has to a large extent been destroyed by the machinations of giant brewing conglomerates. Whitbread's IPA brewed at Castle Eden was made available commercially in cask and bottle as Fuggles Imperial IPA and enjoyed considerable success. But in the late 1990s Whitbread lost interest in small volume beers and then lost all interest in brewing, finally selling to Interbrew of Belgium in 2000. The beer has disappeared. The Samuel Allsopp IPA was never brewed commercially and the Ind Coope plant was bought by Bass in the late 1990s and amalgamated with its own neighbouring site. Marston's has occasionally brewed its IPA but its range of occasional beers was stopped when it was taken over by Wolverhampton & Dudley. It still brews a bottle-conditioned IPA for Tesco supermarkets.

On the credit side, the renowned bottle-conditioned IPA, Worthington White Shield, has returned to Burton-on-Trent after a peripatetic existence for several years. The beer survived the merger of Bass and Worthington in the 1920s, and became a cult drink in the dog days of keg beer and pasteurised bottled beers in the 1950s and 60s. When Bass allowed volumes to slip, it moved the brewing to other parts of its empire and then in the late 1990s licensed the independent family brewery of King & Barnes in Horsham Sussex, to make the beer. When King & Barnes closed in 2000 there were fears that White Shield might die. But Steve Wellington, the brewer at the Museum Brewery within the Bass complex at Burton, brought the beer back home, with the enthusiastic support of Bass executives. The 5.6 per cent ale is brewed from pale and crystal malts with Challenger and Goldings hops. It has 21 units of colour, 40 units of bitterness, a rich malt, sultana fruit and bitter hops aroma and flavour, and a long hoppy finish. Goldings have replaced Northdown in the recipe and, surprisingly, it no longer has a traditional Burton sulphury nose. But it is a superb bottled pale ale and a palpable link with 19th-century Burton brewing.

White Shield, a famous name that evokes 19th-century brewing.

Where pale ale is concerned, history has not repeated itself either as tragedy or farce, to paraphrase Karl Marx's famous phrase. It has simply gone back to its roots. Marston's Pedigree is not offered as an IPA but it is certainly a classic Burton pale ale, made only from pale malt and brewing sugar, with no darker malts. And the Burton Bridge craft brewery in the town offers possibly the finest interpretation of a true IPA. Geoff Mumford and Bruce Wilkinson, who learned their brewing skills with Ind Coope in Burton and Romford, brew their Empire Pale Ale to a powerful 7.5 per cent alcohol by volume. It is made with Pipkin pale malt and invert sugar, with no darker malts, it is hopped with Challenger whole hops and dry hopped with Styrian Goldings. When brewing is complete it is stored in oak casks for three months to reproduce the length of a sea journey from England to Calcutta. The beer, available only in bottle-conditioned form, has a big fruity and peppery aroma, with hops and juicy malt dominating the palate, and a long, dry, hoppy finish that bursts with citrus fruits. All those many years ago, when colonial civil servants and soldiers watched from the docks at Calcutta as the proud sailing ships arrived from London and Liverpool, this was the beer they were waiting for with such eager anticipation.

Sources and further reading

The Brewing Industry in England, 1700-1830, Peter Mathias, Cambridge University Press.

The British Brewing Industry 1830-1989, T R Gourvish and R G Wilson, Cambridge University Press.

A History of Brewing, H S Corran, David & Charles.

The Ale Trail, Roger Protz, Verulam Books.

Papers presented to a seminar on Burton Pale Ales at the White Horse, Parson's Green, London in 1990.

For details of all cask-conditioned and bottle-conditioned ales brewed in Britain see the *Good Beer Guide*, editor Roger Protz (published annually by the Campaign for Real Ale).

For an up-to-date list of many American and Canadian craft-brewed beers see *Best American Beers* by Ben Myers, published in the US and Britain by Quadrillion.

Special thanks to:

Charles McMaster, whose paper on Scottish IPAs presented to the White Horse seminar in 1990 has been most useful in writing the Scottish section.

Malcolm Barr-Hamilton of the London Borough of Tower Hamlets' Local History Library and Archives.

Nicholas Redman, the Whitbread Archive.

Brewing India Pale Ales

by *Clive La Pensée*

Acknowledgements

My thanks go to the Durden Park Beer Circle and especially James McCrorie. Durden Park have made it possible to try to recreate historical beers, not only by their tireless search for original recipes, but also because of their analysis of old brewing methods and the meanings of the terms used.

Any book on Scottish Ales should have been written by James McCrorie. His knowledge and insight has been an inspiration, as has the constructive criticism he applied to my text. I've tried writing on the history of brewing in a vacuum and it's very hard.

Alma Topen of the University of Glasgow Archive always found time to talk me through the things I didn't understand and search out the other half of the bits I only half knew about.

The staff of the British Library are simply brill, friendly and just so organised. They are an example to everyone who is a custodian of our past

And a special thanks to my friends who tasted my IPA brews (dirty work but someone had to do it), my neighbours for putting up with the smell, weekend after weekend, of the wort boiling and my wife, who did both of these things and found time to apply historical rigour to my flights of fancy.

Clive La Pensée Beverley 2001

Introduction

Any writer asked to contribute to the history and brewing of pale ale and India Pale Ale (IPA), must endure a moment of nervousness. Am I up to this? Do I really know enough? Is the literature which I choose to use really reliable, or is it the work of some Victorian crank who just happened to have enough money or political brewing clout, to get himself into print? How shall I judge this? Now that I've confessed my own inhibitions, it is only fair to reveal the philosophy I decided to adopt when writing the history of IPA brewing techniques.

(i)   It is impossible to even guess at the nature of the ingredients used over 150 years ago. Barley, hops, and yeast are living organisms and don't choose to reliably reproduce their characteristics at our convenience, year in and year out. In other words, we don't really know with what the IPA brewers worked, for their raw materials changed from season to season and were different from place to place. There probably was no definitive IPA.

Water is fickle too. Wells only a few hundred metres apart reveal significant differences in their make up. And anyway, it is not reasonable for home-brewers to trawl the countryside, in the hope of finding a particular brewing water.

(ii)   Nor do they need to. If the original brewers used what they had available, why shouldn't we? This is also part of authentic brewing history. It is definitely part of my philosophy on historical brewing.

(iii)   Malt is another thing entirely. You can't make pale ale with dark malt! We do have to try and get close to the real thing, even if that is only in terms of our modern day barley and malt. We know that only very pale malt was used for IPA, much paler than we may be able to purchase nowadays as pale malt. If you can't get hold of a genuine pale malt, there is nothing to stop you making your own malt, or mixing pale and lager malts. I hope you will make your own and so I have included details on how to do this in Appendix 3. Making malt is at least as exciting as making beer.

(iv)   Hops are a nightmare for historical brewers. Nowadays hops come with an alpha acid assay and so we can reliably predict the degree of bittering, which they will render to the beer. Historically we have to do with descriptions such as "Pale Mid-Kent". I have taken note of authorities such as the Durden Park brewers. Fortunately they had already researched this topic and I've adopted their suggestions on some modern day available products as alternatives to the original vagueness. Essentially we are left with Goldings and Fuggles at around 4.5-6% alpha acid as the only realistic alternatives and are those suggested by Durden Park research. The Durden Park Beer Circle have done so much towards researching old beers, that it is maybe they who should really be writing this book. However, knowing and writing are two different things. I am completely indebted to them and offer my writing skills as a contribution to getting a handle on brewing history and making some traditional beers. This is not a cop out! In the final analysis, this is my bit of book and I have sole responsibility for its contents. If you think I've erred, then I do ask you sincerely to offer your corrections.

(v)   Yeast is another problem. It is this fungus, which has the task of converting the maltose solution, which is referred to as the wort, into alcohol and carbon dioxide. It does this in several phases. During the primary fermentation the yeast cells convert sugar and use any oxygen present in the wort to enable the cells to reproduce. This aerobic respiration is essential in order to increase the yeast cell concentration and ensure a good fermentation. Once all the oxygen has been used up by the yeast it will begin to ferment anaerobically, making less carbon dioxide and more alcohol, but not making any more yeast cells. Once all the easily fermentable sugar has been used up, most of the yeast settles out and the beer is run from it into casks. There are still any amount of higher sugars left in the wort, and the actual amount depends on the ability of the yeast strain to keep working under difficult anaerobic conditions coupled with a low sugar concentration. A good IPA yeast must remain active and once in the cask, continue working on the larger molecules, which could not be immediately broken down during the primary fermentation. The barely fermentable molecules are dealt with in the conditioning phase, which is responsible for major changes in the nature of the beer. It is the conditioning phase which takes time and ties up capital and equipment and so is replaced in non-traditional breweries by filtration and pasteurisation to give clarity and shelf life. Even the much admired Continental lager beers receive the same rude treatment.

If at all possible, get a live working yeast from a brewery. If this is not feasible then you will have to do as I do and labour on with dried yeasts. Appendix 4 has a list of yeast culture suppliers and some thoughts on keeping a yeast strain going for a pale ale. It is essential to get a yeast capable of good attenuation, i.e. capable of breaking down all the fermentable material in the wort. It is unlikely that many brewing yeasts of 150 years ago produced the degree of attenuation, which we nowadays regard as normal. That said, we do know that IPA brewers expected to get down to a gravity of around 1012 before casking the beer and brewers such as Roberts in Edinburgh cared for a good strain and enjoyed excellent yeast performance. They helped attenuation by rousing the fermenting beer frequently, because the input of oxygen from the air encourages yeast to keep reproducing and prevents premature flocculation, which takes cells out of circulation.

We know that the dock workers in India also threw a great amount of IPA in the nearest harbour basin as undrinkable. A successful yeast thrives at the expense of other micro-organisms, which ruin beer. In other words, poor yeast leads to ruined beer and nineteenth-century IPA brewers were not always blessed with the strong yeast cultures and sterilising solutions that we now regard as normal.

(vi)   Are we all practiced home brewers, or are there some among us who don't know our gyle from our gaiter? I assume the latter, but as I don't want to try to teach my grandmother (bless her) to suck eggs, I've gone for a compromise, and included a short summary of terms in the body of the text, which I hope won't distract the seasoned brewer, who will want to skip them quickly.

(vii)   Historical terms are dealt with in the main text if to so do sheds light on nineteenth century brewing techniques. My aim is to avoid interrupting the flow of the argument by giving explanations which are for many, unnecessary, whilst still enabling readers who are not committed brewers, to find their way into making an excellent IPA. A glossary of terms is to be found in Appendix 1.

(viii) And finally, the definition. I have rejected many modern IPAs because they no longer adhere to the original *raison d'être* of an India Pale Ale. Nor is there any particular reason why a modern beer should slavishly follow the original concept. Modern brewers have different priorities and don't need to cope with months of shaking in the hold of a ship in tropical heat. So why should they allow for that. Nor am I going to claim that modern IPAs are not excellent beers, but we have to set our stall out and we've decided that an original gravity of 1055 and above and genuinely pale, no grits, very high hopping rates to boot, is our baseline. Some purists would argue that this figure is too low and an OG of at least 1070 is more appropriate. A very high hop rate is the main identifying character of a *true* IPA, plus a long maturation period of at least 12 months, preferably 16 months for a OG of 1070 and at around 75g per 5 litres (2$\frac{1}{2}$ oz per gallon). Goldings hops are required to recreate an original IPA. That was what IPA meant to nineteenth-century brewers.

Pale Ale, Mild Ale and IPA

The Parameters

IPA is really a strong export pale ale. The name would indicate India as the destination, but a glance at Table 1 reveals that by 1840, the United Kingdom and Ireland were exporting beers all over the world. Furthermore we see that this lucrative trade had already reached a crisis by 1842, and was showing signs of an imminent market collapse. The reasons for this have not been easy to explain but I assume that as the numbers of Europeans working in the Colonies increased, it became economically viable to brew in situ. Instead of exporting beer, we exported breweries. Ironically enough, China was a considerable purchaser of English beer in 1841, worth some 2240 barrels. By the turn of the century, one region of it had become a German naval base, which accounts for the picture of my

Above, left: The child is the author's father in law in a photograph taken around 1912 in the Port of Tsingtao. His father was part of the German Navy stationed there.

Right: The Germans exported a brewery and now on your supermarket shelves you can find a perfect copy of a German lager, called Tsingtao Beer from the Tsingtao Brewery Company Ltd. of China.

father in law in our possession, taken around 1912 in the Port of Tsingtao. He is in infant clothing and with a Chinese nanny. His father was part of the German Navy stationed there and family lore has it, he was a chum of Admiral Tirpitz. The Germans were not in a position to export enough Pilsner to such a far flung region, so they exported a brewery instead and now on my supermarket shelves I find a perfect copy of a German lager, called Tsingtao Beer from the Tsingtao Brewery Company Ltd. of China. It's also the star turn in our local Chinese Restaurant as is the Indian lager, now available a few doors up in my local Bangladeshi restaurant. It probably has a similar history to Tsingtao Beer.

The letters IPA are synonymous with strong powerfully flavoured pale export ales. I wonder what the Chinese and Indian brewers use to define their export to us. May I suggest BBL (Bland British Lager). Certainly, the British export to the East of 150 years ago was a finer thing than that which we now import.

IPA was brewed stronger than many ales brewed for the home market in order that it would be able to withstand the rigours of a long sea journey in climes far too warm for thin beer to survive. It wasn't the strongest beer around at the time and certainly had a good pedigree from some fearsome domestic pale ales, for which the nineteenth century was justly famous. The high alcohol content helped inhibit bacterial growth within the beer, which may otherwise have ruined it. Similarly, high hopping rates were used as the disinfecting character of hops was already well understood by brewers. Hop amounts were frequently used that would have produced an extremely bitter beer, but that was something which the colonial drinkers seemed prepared to put up with, although we must always remember that bittering mellows with time and produces some quite exquisite flavours. As we shall see, once their taste buds had adjusted, the Empire may have ended up demanding these fantastic beers.

In these giddy days of being hide bound by beer styles, it is refreshing to read an 1868 definition of a pale ale. I paraphrase from *The Brewer: A familiar treatise on the art of Brewing* and other sources. Please remember that any description is likely to be a generalisation, and you won't have to look far in brewing literature or brewing opinion, in order to find someone to contradict what I've distilled out. But one has to stop somewhere.

(i)   Colour was important. It had to be very pale, and made from only the finest malts. Until recently it was probably nearly impossible to get the right malt for a genuine pale ale. I fre-

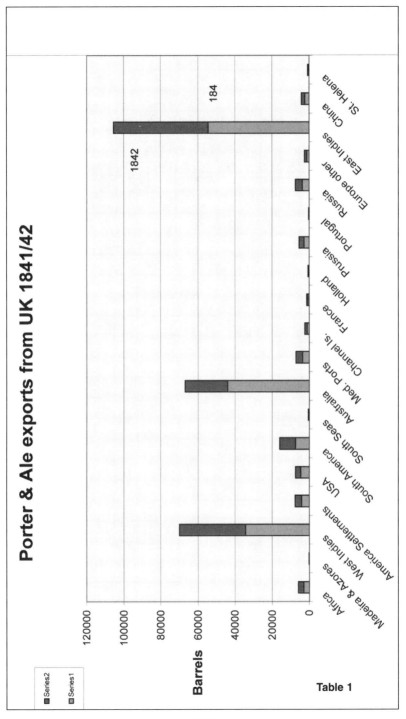

Porter & Ale exports from UK 1841/42

quently brew pale ales using British Maris Otter pale malt. The Ale tastes and looks beautiful but is anything but pale. A mixture of pale and lager malts does the trick but it isn't a compromise with which I feel comfortable. Any darker malts were seen as an adulteration. Beestons Maltings may continue producing a malt which seems close to the original product. Whitbread Breweries always made the return "White Malt," for IPA. White malt was not roasted at all for colour and notes for making this now lost malt type are included in Appendix 3.

(i)   Ordinary pale ale should have less body than bitter ales but paradoxically, they were sometimes higher in hops to the extent that when reading the recipes we may expect the beer to resemble a medicinal tonic rather than a popular beverage. We mustn't be diverted by such suppositions.

(iii)   Mild Ale differs from pale ale in being somewhat sweeter, some-what stronger in alcohol and having no marked predominance of the flavour or smell of hops. Mild was often termed "home-brewed ale". The term "mild" was only an indication of low hopping rates and didn't differ substantially from other strong ales. It is this lack of hop character which defines a mild as opposed to bitter.

Here is an 1860s mild ale recipe. The method was general for all ales and especially for strong pale ales.

RECIPE 1 (HISTORICAL)

VICTORIAN ALE RECIPE

Method for an Ordinary Domestic Mild Ale.
Domestic Brewer 1860

I give this recipe in its original form. It was written for the small house brewer and hence contains detail that we normally miss when brews are written up for professionals. Note the difference between a Victorian mild ale and pale ale (given in brackets).

ORIGINAL GRAVITY   1067 (1097)   17° (24°) PLATO

WATER   No water analysis

	25 LITRES	23 LITRES	5 UK GALS	5 US GALS
Pale Malt	6.1 kg	5.6 kg	12.3 lb	10 lb

COPPER HOPS
Goldings 5% alpha-acid. Sometimes left over from a highly hopped brew on a previous day.

	95 g	85 g	3.2 oz	2.6 oz

BREWING METHOD

- Let the malt be crushed the day before mashing, and kept ready in dry sacks.
- At 5 o'clock morning, light fire under copper and bring liquor to boil; allow to boil gently a quarter of an hour.
- At 7 o'clock run into mash tun, a barrel and a half of liquor just off the boil and when cooled down to 168°F (75°C), add the grist by degrees, briskly stirring all the time.
- After the whole of the malt has been put in, continue the mashing for at least half an hour, and then turn on, from under the false bottom of the tun, one barrel more liquor at 180°F (82°C), keeping up the heat (in the copper) to 185°F (85°C).
- Prolong the mashing for three quarters of an hour, cover up close and let the goods stand two hours, after which set the tap, sparging on at the same time half a barrel of liquor at 190°F (88°C).
- *Omit the sparge for a pale ale of 1097 gravity.*
- Let all this be drawn off pretty close, when there should be two barrels of wort in the underback. Pump up immediately into wort-copper.
- Next shut off the draining taps and mash again fifteen minutes with two barrels of liquor at 190°F (88°C).
- All the liquor required will now have been used, and the second wort, if the malt be good, should, when fully drawn off, yield $2\frac{3}{4}$ barrels in the underback.

- If the wort copper is large enough to contain and boil the produce of two mashings at one time, with the whole of the hops, so much the better; if not, the first two barrels, the gravity of which ought to be 32 lb per barrel, may be boiled an hour and a quarter, with nearly four-fifths of the hops, that is $3\frac{3}{4}$ lb. The second wort of $2\frac{3}{4}$ barrels at the gravity of eight to nine lb per barrel should then be boiled two hours with the remainder of the hops viz. $1\frac{1}{4}$ lb.

- After straining from the hops and cooling and combining the worts there should be $3\frac{1}{2}$ barrels at 24 lb per barrel.

ALCOHOL CONTENT	6.5% v/v	5.1% w/w

BITTERNESS: 38 EBU

COLOUR: 4.0 EBC

COMMENTS

Mild ales were pale in colour and only differed from pale ales in the hop amounts used. This wouldn't have been considered a keeping ale, because of the moderate bittering. It was not uncommon to make an IPA on one day and then use the massive amounts of hops to flavour a mild ale on the next. Nowadays we think of mild ales as being darker in colour, almost on the way to being a brown, but this was not typical 150 years ago.

This particular recipe also gives the following advice: "A pale ale should follow the same directions but the sparge be reduced to give a wort of gravity 35lb per barrel (OG 1097, 24°P).

This is one of my favourite pale ale recipes, although, in keeping with pale ale tradition, I use at least double the hop amounts.

A Gentleman's Art

At the beginning of the nineteenth century, there were nearly as many methods of brewing beer as there were breweries. By the time IPA came to be a popular drink at home and abroad, it was possible to buy standardised brewing equipment and thus with time many brewers were making their beer in very similar ways to their neighbours. Existing plant was, of course, often retained for reasons of economy, and when we read of some quite quirky brews, these may have more to do with idiosyncrasies of the brew house, than any conviction that it was good practice. This is most important to remember, especially as brewers may have been very conservative and reluctant to move with the times. Recipes dated 1850 may well have been around in a country house brewery for generations.

The above method, with a combination of sparging and double mashing, and over and under mashing seems to be about the average method for the period when IPA was in its fullest bloom. Most breweries went for either bottom or top mashing or for double mashes or sparges. This recipe shows how reluctant some breweries were to make a decision on what they thought most efficacious, so they kept doing a bit of everything. We can use this mild ale recipe to help us understand the techniques that were around at the beginning of the nineteenth century.

The beer was still mashed in a wood or metal tun with a false perforated bottom. There was a boiler, usually referred to as the copper (nowadays often referred to as the hot liquor tank), situated above the mash tun to enable a gravity feed of hot water into the mash tun. Sometimes there was also an over back for holding or boiling liquor. Underneath the mash tun was an underback. I'm indebted to Dr. Sambrook for finally providing the origin of "back". It essentially derives from "buck" which we now know as "bucket". Hence the underback is a container for catching run off from the mash tun. The overback would be a container above the mash tun for holding the wort until the boiler was available to boil it. This problem can be solved by modern home-brewers by simply utilising a second boiler, situated lower than the mash tun. Diagram 1 (over the page) shows a drawing of my 10 gallon house-brewery, which I've modelled on a nineteenth-century cottage brewery, lifted from the Loudon design from 1833. The design changes for modern-day uses are discussed in *The Craft of House-Brewing*.

I doubt many households in the nineteenth century brewed in ten gallon lots. Beer was a reliable source of liquid intake, and so was

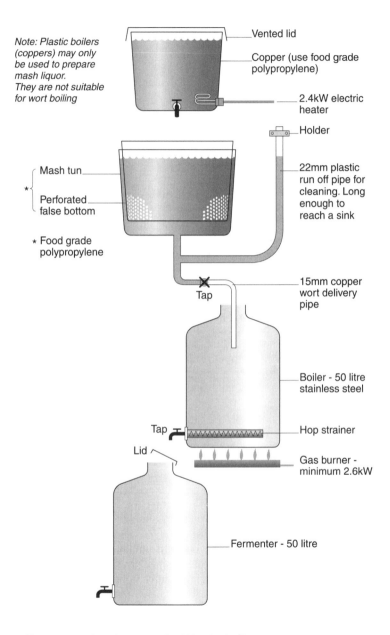

Note: Plastic boilers (coppers) may only be used to prepare mash liquor. They are not suitable for wort boiling

Vented lid

Copper (use food grade polypropylene)

2.4kW electric heater

Holder

Mash tun

* { Perforated false bottom

* Food grade polypropylene

22mm plastic run off pipe for cleaning. Long enough to reach a sink

15mm copper wort delivery pipe

Tap

Boiler - 50 litre stainless steel

Tap

Hop strainer

Lid

Gas burner - minimum 2.6kW

Fermenter - 50 litre

The water supply to the copper should be plumbed in.
Water pumps driven by an electric drill work well too if the water has to be lifted.

brewed and consumed in huge quantities. The principle remains the same for 10 gallons or 10 barrels. We now try to avoid the use of raw wood and brick as these materials are impossible to keep sterile. By the 1830s most commercial brewers were utilising iron and copper.

Our original IPA brewers fought a constant battle to maintain hygiene, and thus prevent beer infections. To solve such problems now we use food grade polypropylene for the low temperature tuns and stainless steel for the boiler. The copper is heated using electricity, but for regulated heating, it is handy to have a gas heated boiler (a kind of gas fired underback), which serves to hold the wort and to boil it, and so eliminate pumping the wort back up to the copper. This allows good temperature control and so avoids caramelisation of the sugars in the wort.

Only more sophisticated nineteenth-century breweries had an underback which doubled as a second copper. Once the wort was run off into the underback it was commonly hand pumped back to the copper above the mash tun for boiling.

The nineteenth century saw the introduction of run-off pipes, which could put the water into the grist from under the false bottom. This was called bottom mashing or turning the goods under, and apart from aiding mixing the mash, this technique floated fine particles to the top, where they wouldn't block the perforated floor. It also reduced the risk of splashing and scalding, which was always attendant when top mashing, which involves running water onto the top of the grist, or pouring the malt into hot water, and trying to stir at the same time. Bottom mashing was already well established as a technique by the nineteenth century. Sambrook found reference to it as early as 1635 and it is fair to assume that most major IPA producers were employing a perforated false bottom in their mash tun and were running the water in from the bottom. Bottom mashing was however by no means universally employed by 1830, and some writers gave the option of "turning under or over" in IPA recipes much later than 1840. Loudon referred to it as a new invention as late as 1845. According to Sambrook's research, brewers claimed the worts from bottom mashing " were quicker and freer, and the flavour more delicate."

I'm still amazed how few modern home-brewers bottom mash, despite the common use of perforated false bottoms in the mash tun. Any serious brewer of historical nineteenth century ales must consider this option, although many original IPA brewers, as shown in our mild/pale ale recipe above, still used a mixture of the two. Old habits died hard and I'm sure brewers wanted to hedge their bets! Mashing 10 quarters of malt by a new method, takes courage, and that is the name of a famous nineteenth century brewery.

Some breweries already had mechanised mashers, which used steam power to rotate a mashing cylinder placed horizontally across the main tun. The grist and water were first mixed in this contraption which for all intents and purposes sounds as if it must have had its origins in the building industry as a cement mixer. "The Steels Masher" was apparently more akin to a meat mincer. The drum didn't rotate, but a worm screw inside turned and pushed the grist through the barrel, where it was injected with hot water. By the end of its travel the malt was well wetted and had the right porridge-like consistency, so it was allowed to fall into the mash tun.

Without any form of mixing device it must have been a miserable existence for brewers. Firstly they had to crush maybe 150 kg (8 bushels) of malt, which would have been a modest brew and then hand pump up, and stoke up the copper to heat 40 gallons of hot water. Once heated to 75°C (166°F) the water was run down onto the grain. By now the brewhouse was probably like a sauna, but the goods still had to be mashed for an hour. Unlike our modern use of the word, in the nineteenth century, mashed meant just that. He stirred the goods with a large oar for up to one or more hours.

Before mashing could commence, the brewer or his apprentice had to put out the copper fire or get some water pumped up into the now empty copper, before it ruined. Once the plant was safe, he grabbed an oar and started the back-breaking task of mixing the malt and water.

After an hour of this hot and dangerous work, he maybe got an hour for rest, while the goods infused, but more likely the copper needed stoking up to prepare the sparge water in a Scottish brewery or the second mash liquor if South of the Border. Once the sparge or second mash was finished he stoked again to receive the combined worts for boiling, which he still had to pump back up from the underback. Very often the copper was not large enough to hold the total amount of liquor which had been run through the goods, and so the worts had to be boiled in several batches, a process which could easily take several hours per wort.

The sparge required careful tap control if an effective extraction was to be achieved, hence the popularity of multiple mashing. It was far easier to run the wort into the underback and then run in another charge of hot water for a second mash. While this second wort was infusing, the first wort was pumped back up into the copper and the fire stoked up for boiling. Nevertheless the day of the sparge arrived about the time that IPA brewing was at its height and as it was a Scottish thing, I'll deal with it under Scottish beers.

Brewing was considered a gentleman's art in the 18th century, but we may be sure the gentlemen who brewed employed a labourer for this awful and exacting work.

Once the wort was back in the copper it had to be boiled for at least one hour but needed careful attention to prevent a too hot fire causing burning or foaming over, or a too small fire allowing the beer to go off the boil. During this time, the hops may have been added to the boil, or they were prepared in the underback for the hot wort to be run onto them. Frequently both options were used. The underback may also have run onto large iron or wooden trays, to cool the wort quickly. Either option influenced the nature of the beer, for hot wort oxidises in air and neither iron nor wood are neutral materials and certainly effected the flavour.

The underback may itself have served as a fermenter but this was not good practice as it tied up the whole brewery for several days until fermentation was finished. Once safely in the fermenter, the yeast was pitched and care taken to keep air out, which could carry wild yeast or bacteria capable of ruining a beer. Unfortunately, as desirable as hygiene is, yeast won't ferment the sugar to alcohol very successfully, unless it starts life in an oxygenated environment, which it needs in order to reproduce. The wort is by now devoid of oxygen, and an anaerobic fermentation causes the yeast to struggle through life surviving on the wrong set of chemical reactions, which give the beer any number of odd side tastes. So the brewer roused his fermentation regularly to supply the much needed oxygen and prevent premature settling out of the yeast. Amsinck was a firm advocate of rousing. Light ales (OG less than 1045) were roused 24 hours after pitching until within 12 hours of skimming or cleansing the wort of the yeast. Strong ales were roused 36 hours after pitching.

The *Domestic Brewer* of 1860 records:

- "The first wort for a strong ale should be pitched at 59°F with $1^1/_2$ lb yeast per barrel.

- Do not let the heat rise above 75°F. Attenuate down to one third the original gravity and skim off the head every two hours, until it almost ceases to rise.

- After the second day, it will generally be found requisite to rouse strong worts continually, perhaps every three hours, in order to quicken the fermentation and carry the attenuation sufficiently low within a reasonable time."

We may choose not to rouse the beer during fermentation as we have many more elegant methods of getting oxygen into the wort, without risking infection by stirring an open fermenter. Most modern brewers use some form of pump arrangement to bubble air into the wort and aerate it. This air is usually firstly drawn through a sterile filter. I draw it through a length of copper tubing which is flash heated in a gas flame. Another method I can recommend to small scale brewers is to bubble all air which enters any vat through sterilising solution. Sodium metabisulphite is good, because it does not froth. However, the air needs washing in a second trap, with clean water, to prevent sulphur dioxide entering the wort. If proprietary sterilising solution is to be used in the first trap, a second empty trap will be needed to catch the froth and prevent it entering the liquor. A more elegant solution is to use dry micron air-filters, available through any home-brew retailer stocking Brupaks' merchandise.

Historically worts were always being lost due to infection, lacto-bacilli being the most common microbe to spread havoc. Nineteenth-century brewers even tried to make a virtue out of sour beer and some minor continental breweries still manage to sell infected beer at an inflated price and convince the drinker it tastes great. It all reminds me of the parable of the King and his invisible suit of clothes that only wise men could see, but to be fair, the Flemish brewers really do understand how to impart the faintest suspicion of flavour.

Some house breweries are still blighted by the sour beer problem and once it has taken hold, only a thorough hose out with dilute bleach solution will rid a brewery of it! I have to mash, transfer liquor, boil, ferment and serve in the same 3.4m². Splashes and spillages are impossible to avoid and create a perfect breeding ground for lacto-bacilli. I probably can't permanently rid my brewery of all the lacto-bacilli colonies, so once the wort has been boiled with the hops, all air entering the wort container or fermenter, has to pass through some form of sterilising process.

Once saturated with air, the pump is turned off and the yeast pitched. Neither of these methods will have the same effect on the fermentation as rousing the wort every few hours. This continuous rousing means that aerobic fermentation can continue, whereas the modern method is to allow aerobic fermentation long enough to get a good concentration of working yeast, and then starve the yeast of oxygen, as anaerobic fermentation wastes less sugar in producing carbon dioxide. I have no problem with rousing, except that it allows infected air into the fermenter. Hence I switch the air pump on regularly to give the same effect as a rouse. Working brewers who can't afford to give up the day job, will help themselves with some form of timer switch.

In well constructed breweries, the fermentation took place outside the mash area in order to reduce the problems of cross infection. The mash and boiler room were hot, wet and spillage of wort was even more unavoidable then than now. It too was the perfect place for lactobacilli to flourish and send a fermentation sour. If the brewhouse was also used for fermenting, it had to be well enough ventilated, to drop the temperature to around 13°C (55°F) after the excesses of heating the mash water, sparge water and boiling the wort. As mentioned, some primitive country house breweries used the mash tun or the underback as a fermenting vat. This also tied up the whole brewery and prevented another brew from being started. It was thus more common to ferment in a separate cellar, and by judicious use of lead pipe, which carried the wort outside the brewery buildings, the wort was cooled on its way to the cellar. We nowadays reject lead on grounds of safety and use copper. Being thinner walled it works much better than lead but, unless using compression joints, be sure to ask your plumber's merchant for lead free solder. It works just as well as the leaded variety.

Quality beers were, and still should be, only brewed between October and March, so the rate of wort cooling was worth the effort and expense of the lead pipe.

Once fermented, the young beer was casked and matured until ready to drink. This conditioning phase can take twelve months or more in a strong beer. Strong beers of the IPA type had to be ready for a long journey, taking many months. IPAs were kept a summer and then casked or bottled after most of the dissolved carbon dioxide had evolved. This reduced the risk of the cask blowing during the voyage. The weaker domestic ales needed between six months and one year. This long maturation was in part caused by the extreme hopping ratios. With time the hop harshness abates and even a very highly-hopped IPA eventually ceases to strip the cheek cells. That moment, when a hoppy beer is no longer harsh but still retains its hoppiness, is the moment of supreme joy to an IPA drinker.

Brewer's Wisdom

Rules of thumb abound in beer literature. I could write a whole book just on diversities of method and that fact is worth bearing in mind when trying to brew an authentic IPA. When your style judge turns up his or her nose and says, "That's not IPA!" stay calm in the knowledge it probably was once upon a time an IPA to someone, somewhere. Beer styles have surely done more to ruin an amateur brewer's joy in his craft than any other single thing. Please, don't spend your life jumping over your own shadow wondering if this or that is a genuine IPA. Enjoy the fruits of your labour instead.

So here are the rules of thumb, taken from *The Brewer*, of 1868. This is quite late in IPA terms and brewing technology had progressed enough to eliminate the quirkier notions that had been around earlier that century.

- Temperature ranges. Pale malts were mashed at 70°C (158°F), darker malts up to 76°C (170°F). 74°C (165°F) was a good middle value, less than 63°C (145°F) was considered useless. Amsinck altered his mash temperatures according to water hardness. He mashed soft waters at least 2°F lower than a hard water. All the above values are considered too high nowadays, when one would be reluctant to err from between 63–68°C (145–154°F), but nowadays everyone seems to mash for extract. However, mashing then was not what it is now. The goods were stirred for anything up to an hour and then rested. The stirring process was called mashing and the time for the infusion referred to as resting. Remember that both these phases are now referred to as mashing. Hence the given temperatures should be seen more as strike temperatures.

- The ambient temperature was between 13–15°C (50–55°F) to facilitate cooling the wort.

- 0.5 kg (1lb) malt at 13°C (50°F) mixed with 0.5 kg (1 lb) water at 82°C (180°F) was thought to settle out at 41°C (105°F).

- The tap temperature at run off was between 60–66°C (140–150°F). This was considered the all important value, probably because it was easiest to measure. This is what we would now refer to as a mash temperature.

- A lower temperature produced a poor conversion. Higher tap temperatures damaged the diastase, which are the enzyme group which convert starch to fermentable maltose. High mash temperatures may well have been used to produce a different quality to the beer. "Mash cool for alcohol and hot for flavour," is one rule of thumb that seems to have little credence now but I'm sure it is worth regarding. Mashes at over 70°C (155°F) can be quite stunning and are a technique open to house brewers, who do not have to concern themselves with price and profitability.

- A good dense close froth on run off was considered a good indication that a correct heat had been applied and good conversion achieved.

- The first liquor to run off was returned to the top of the goods to remove any solid material. Many craft brewers still return the liquor from the tap run off to the top of the mash tun until it runs through clear.

- If second and third mashes were used, the water was run on at 82°C and 93°C respectively (180°F and 200°F)

- Sparge water was run on at 82°C (180°F).

- Export beer needed exceptionally large amount of hops to enable it to survive the long sea journey. Pale ale was hopped at a rate of 66g per 20 litres (2.4 oz per $4\frac{1}{2}$ gallon) brew. India Ales were hopped at around twice that rate.

- Fermenting temperatures were around 13 –15 °C (56–64°F)

- Up to around 1850 Scottish brewers fermented much more slowly. They eventually became victims of their own success and were required to produce so much beer that after that date they tended towards English temperatures.

- "Keeping beers" were always strong beers (in terms of alcohol) and were therefore suitable as export beers. The antiseptic powers of the alcohol were appreciated if not understood. Strong March beers were also used to blend with weaker beers brewed during the summer months and what was left over was sold in autumn as Old Ale.

- Weak beers depended only on the hops for keeping and soured more easily.

- Mild ales depended mainly on alcohol for keeping.

- IPAs used hops and alcohol to survive the long journeys.

- Pale ale was given to yeast bite, due to the long cool fermentations. This was thought to have been caused by keeping the lid on during boiling and was supposed to "leave a nauseous bitter taste lingering on the palate, apt to cause the beer to stupefy and give headaches." I've no idea if this has any basis in reality. It is a point which needs researching and contrasting with modern day continental pressure fermentations which are done in sealed vessels with a pressure safety valve!

Times and fashions are just as active in brewing as elsewhere. That must be remembered when accepting or rejecting any notion on historical or modern brewing. Everyone had/has an axe to grind.

Mashing an IPA

The mashing process is probably the single most important process carried out by the brewer. Its object is to convert a plant's natural reserves from starch into fermentable sugar. All plants spend most of the summer converting carbon dioxide into starch using only sunlight and a bit of water. We harvest them, often as the seed, and use this starch, put by as an energy store for the next generation of plants to germinate, as an energy source to sustain our life.

The plants cannot use starch directly as an energy supply, and so they have to convert it firstly into soluble sugars. For this they use complicated molecules called enzymes. The brewer has long appreciated how the enzymes used in nature's process can be used to make sugars, which can be fermented to yield alcohol, thousands of years before he understood the process. Not only does our hobby descend from the second oldest profession, but mashing is also the father and mother of modern biochemistry, it having been the first to be comprehended by scientists and then rationalised to make best use of nature's arts.

Only warmth and the universal transport medium, water, are needed along with a strong paddle, oar or stout spoon to get a homogeneous mix of the grain in the water, and restart the starch to sugar conversion. Strictly speaking only this mixing process is called "mashing," the goods then being left or "rested" once they have been thoroughly mixed. As mentioned, modern house brewers now tend to refer to both the mixing and resting as "mashing".

It is all the more surprising then that mashing, a fairly straightforward and well understood process, should be the subject of so much discussion, and although mashing was the first biochemical process to be thoroughly researched and understood, prior to being rationalised in an industrial process, history has still yielded the modern day small-scale house brewer dozens of mash techniques for a variety of beers. We can afford to indulge ourselves with a multitude of methods long since rejected by the rationalisation lobby. Even restricting ourselves to Pale and India Pale Ales leaves us with a diversity of methods to consider. Should the water be run in from underneath the grain, (bottom mashing) or poured onto the grain or stirred with the grain as both are poured together into the mash tun, or as many Craft Brewers prefer, the grist be added and mashed into the hot liquor etc.? Should the water be hot, so that the grain immediately settles out at the correct mash temperature, or cold, and be brought up to the correct temperature by the addition of hot water, or by using some external heat, and should it be brought to the correct heat rapidly or in steps and with frequent rests?

The diversity seems endless, and the reason for this plethora of methods is that each technique yields a different product, or copes with a peculiarity of a certain type of malt, or is suited to a particular design of brewery or last but not least, suited a simply downright quirky or eccentric brewer.

And of course we have to deal with descriptions, which may have seemed perfectly obvious back in 1839, but seem to have little logic or make no sense to us today. Here, for example is a recipe for a pale ale from *Domestic Brewing; a hand book for families 1839*. It is certainly much older than the date it was recorded, which pre-dated the thermometer and it serves as a good starting point when trying to understand the needs of a pale ale brewer over two hundred years ago.

RECIPE 2 (HISTORICAL)

SHROPSHIRE PALE ALE

Domestic Brewing *1839*

See Recipe 3 for a Homebrew version of this recipe.

Ingredients for 36 gallons

5.5 bushels malt

Worcestershire hops 1.25 lb/bushel

- Mash 1 bushel at a time using as much water at the usual temperature as is needed to wet goods.
- When thoroughly wetted, pour on 15 gallons of boiling water. Rest 3 hours.
- Run off liquor onto the hops already in the cooler.
- Pour back on 12 gallons boiling water.
- Rest 1 hour. Run off.
- Pour on 8 gallons boiling water. Run off. Should have 40 gallons of wort.
- Boil 1 hour.
- Strain through hair sieves into coolers.
- When cool, start yeast and leave overnight in 6 gallons of wort.
- Add the rest of the liquor in 12 hour intervals over the next day.
- Stand 8–10 days.
- Rack into a new keg.
- Add 3 quarts of hot hops which have been infused in boiling water.
- Stop the barrel closely and cover the bung with wet sand.

Now the question is, "Why bother with such descriptions?" In order to understand pale ale and the reasons why its transition to Export and India Ale happened the way it did, we need to delve back to the beginning of the nineteenth century and look at where it all started. Before then, brewers managed without a hydrometer and assumed quite naturally, that the more colour one extracted from malt, the stronger the beer was. The invention or intervention of the hydrometer squashed that notion and brewers quickly realised that dark malts are pretty much a waste of money. They do not yield much extract because pyrolised starch cannot be converted to fermentable sugars. Brewers may have continued to use dark malts for flavour or colour, but I suspect it was more out of convenience. Before plastic bags, it was always a problem to keep a malt in good condition. Malt is naturally hygroscopic and goes slack. Slack malt makes awful beer but slack malt can be roasted a second time to make it into dark malt and can then be used to stretch a good malt. But that was an emergency solution to a serious economic problem and given a choice, brewers were desperate to get away from making dark beers and use pale malts to maximise their profits.

And now comes the fascinating exercise of converting the above recipe into one, which we can use. Beware! We can never recreate that ale! We know too little about the hops, malt and yeast, but what we make is as genuine as anything made two hundred years ago, because the hops, malt and yeast used by those old brewers, were never consistent anyway. They brewed with their technique and enjoyed the variety that evolved season for season.

We also need to take a guess at what the initial strike temperature was. He wetted the malt at the usual temperature and I assume that was around 35–45°C. This would be some kind of protein rest, much the way continental brewers still do when carrying out a decoction mash. It could also have been the temperature at which the brewer just could not keep his hand in the water, i.e. around 60°C.

The temperature was then raised to around 65°C by the addition of hot water. This was not the most common method in later ales but there are plenty of IPA recipes which start off, "Wet the grist in the usual way. Add a barrel of hot water to bring it up to temperature."

The later the recipe, the more likely that the mash water will be heated to around 75°C (167°F), and run onto the grist so that after thorough stirring (mashing) the temperature settles out at around 68°C (154°F). This strike temperature is often much higher in Victorian recipes than we accept nowadays and the strike temperature will affect the beer decisively. Recipes are confusing to us, often giving a copper temperature, tun temperature and tap temperature. Over the years, I've decided to rely much more on the tap temperature, that is the temperature of the wort as it is run out the mash tun. This temperature is more in line with modern mash temperatures. The tun temperature was probably fairly hit-and-miss as it must have been difficult to measure safely and despite all the stirring that went on during what was called mashing, there were certainly still considerable temperature gradients within the goods.

Regular house brewers will also be perplexed by the absence of a hop boil and where is the sparge? Where does the bittering come from. Suddenly brewing an original IPA or pale ale seems a lot more interesting, not to say downright wacky, when done on strict historical principles. It is true that I have decided to start with a recipe which seems to bear very little resemblance to modern day techniques, but it was just such a recipe which gave birth to our modern idea of IPA. Dare we ignore it?

The Sparge and the Boil

The function of the sparge is to rinse the spent grain and thereby extract any residual sugar from within the remaining corn substance. The sparge is done in breweries by long perforated arms rotating above the goods and releasing a fine spray of water over the grain. The grain should not flood as the water will simply channel away down the sides of the vessel. The cake of grain must be carefully formed or else the water finds channels within the grain to drain through. The husks from the grain must be induced to settle out and form a filter bed at the bottom of the mash tun. Should the farinaceous material settle out first, it blocks the perforated false bottom of the mash tun and invariably stops the wort draining. Gallons of hot wort stuck in the spent grains is every brewer's nightmare and it only needs to happen the once, and you take great care to prevent a repetition.

All of these problems are soluble and sparges do work remarkably well, considering the pitfalls that seem inherent in the method. It has to be said that the double mash is far easier. If the mash is the right consistency and has been stirred with attention, the wort runs off without any problem and one doesn't have to regulate the water flow into the tun via the sparge arm, which is always a nuisance if flooding is to be avoided.

In fact the above method of using several mashes instead of sparging was the approved method of brewing in England up until the 1870s. Scottish brewers had already gone over to rinsing techniques, which we now refer to as sparging. Sparging is at least as effective in extracting brewing material as using several mashes. I hesitate to claim it is more effective in a kitchen or outhouse but the commercial guys love sparging for being closer to a continuous brewing system. Brewers have always cursed their luck that brewing only lends itself to batches!

Amsinck isn't precise as to why he disapproves of a one-mash system such as we prefer today. He never allowed himself more than the luxury of using half of his second mash as a final sparge. Regardless of the method used, all brewers were insistent on the need to keep the goods warm and wet in between the various mashes, and thus inhibit mould or bacterial infection of the goods. As we probably won't brew a second weaker beer with the later, thinner worts, which was what the nineteenth-century brewers did, such caution is probably not necessary.

The Scottish system was to sparge until the gyle volume was obtained, which is now a common method on the Continent for their lager style beers and has been adopted by most, if not all UK commercial breweries. One of the Guinness dynasty – actually the nephew to the great man, swore by sparging. I suspect that most home-brew mashers don't sparge with the full gyle amount. It is difficult to move and boil such large volumes and you have to do an open boil to remove quite a lot of the water, if you are to have much say in the starting gravity of the fermentation.

Most of us nowadays heat with gas or electricity, so there is only the cost factor and ducting away of excess steam as arguments against an open boil. Amsinck dismissed electricity as a novelty which would never catch on, and probably boiled over wood or coal most of the time. I'm sure we would be much more tempted to cover our boil, just as Amsinck and his contemporaries did, if we still had to gather wood or shovel coal! And to be fair to Amsinck, he wasn't the only person who should have known better than be rude about electricity. Some years before, the then Prime Minister is reputed to have asked Faraday if electrical induction would actually ever have a use!

Many modern small brewers insist that an open boil is thoroughly beneficial to the final beer, as unpleasant side tastes, which the hops are alleged to incur, can be avoided by steam distilling out unwanted hop components. Open boiling does cause the beer to darken, presumably due to some oxidation, although large amounts of oxygen won't be able to find their way into a boiling wort tun, but mainly due to caramelisation. Open boiling means that a much more substantial heating element or gas flame is needed. Although the overall temperature of the boiling wort may not change that much, the wort near the hot surface will inevitably be darkened as the sugars burn a little. This is not good in a pale ale or IPA, although Amsinck reports that Burton Brewers preferred an open boil as it added colour! Don't assume he was not referring to IPA brewing. The idea of colour in IPA seems to have caused a shudder of disgust in serious brewers, but that doesn't mean that there weren't brewers around who didn't tolerate a darker beer. Remember, pale ales are the hardest to brew. There is nowhere to hide! A little darkness covers a multitude of sins and brewers throughout history have been famous for their pragmatism. One more reason to treat beer "styles" with caution.

Many brewers used a domed base to their copper. This increased the surface area of metal in contact with the wort and allowed a bigger fire to be used without the risk of caramelisation. As we no longer use wood or coal for firing, and gas offers exact heat control, we shan't need to dome our bottoms, but if you do favour a vigorous boil and suffer from wort darkening, a dome will help. Beware the home-brew retailers who offer electric heating for the wort boil. Such boilers must have proper high surface area heaters, and even then, most don't offer proper thermostatic control. Kettle elements get too hot and definitely cause caramelisation and they often overheat, mainly due to hop flowers clogging them, and shut off. This is quite unsuit-

Legend:
- Year 1841
- Year 1842

Barrels axis: 0, 20000, 40000, 60000, 80000, 100000, 120000, 140000, 160000

Country axis: England & Wales, Scotland, Ireland, Allsop & Son

Table 2

able, as it is essential to know the wort has been boiled long enough to reach the hot break. A solution to this problem is to cover the elements with some kind of shield or perforated protection in order to prevent the hops clogging the element and causing overheating. Burco Boilers achieve this.

Our Shropshire Ale is never actually boiled with the hops. The hot liquor, probably around 60°C (140°F) was run onto the hops. This is not copper hopping and will not isomerise much of the bittering component. It is much closer to dry hopping and will extract mainly the aromatic oils, which are otherwise largely boiled off. The main bittering hops are boiled in water to isomerise the bittering acids and then added to the wort prior to fermenting. This may have been because the hops were so unreliable and varied season to season so much in their bittering qualities, it was safer to make up an extract, test it and then add as much as was deemed appropriate.

But I still haven't answered the question, "Sparge or repeat mash?"

The Scots and Irish sparged and the English it seems hung on to their multiple mash system. One way to make up our minds as to which of these is the most authentic method, is to look at the relative amounts of ale and porter being exported to various parts of the world around 1840(see Table 2).

It seems that the two mash English system was the biggest producer of IPA and so that may be the most authentic method to use. That said, Scottish IPA has always been recommended for its quality and the two-mash system did eventually have to give way. For this reason I have separated the English and Scottish methods and included details of the Scottish sparge at the start of the Scottish recipes. I have been warned by some patriotic and sensitive Scots that the figures used to generate Table 2 may be unreliable. This is based on the fact that William Younger shipped beer each week from Leith to London. There it was stored in their warehouse (under Hungerford Bridge) where they had their own wharf. From there it was either supplied to their London retail outlets or taken by barge down to be loaded on ships in the Pool of London about to depart for foreign shores. This beer may have appeared as if 'exported' from London. More research please!

It is worth pointing out that many home-brewers, who by definition are working on a very small scale, find sparging often presents the most intractable problems. Our technology is still as primitive as many small breweries of the last century and I find that the two mash system clears many sparging problems away. One would have to admit that the Scottish and Irish breweries were simply much more up with the modern technology of their time and the English were lagging behind, but that may be too simple. Table 2 shows that the London Brewers Allsop were nearly as successful at exporting Ale and Porter as all the Scottish breweries together. Was the English system really the best, and the one which we should emulate most closely or were Allsop merely good at marketing? How much of their IPA was actually brewed in London? All the later Allsop IPAs were actually brewed in Burton, so we again have to worry about the statistics. Was their geographical position in London such a huge advantage in the export market that they chose to call it a London Beer or was their IPA so much better than all the others, that they managed to brew and export nearly as much as everyone North of the Border? More research needed I feel, but my gut feeling is that market position led to market share and had little to do with quality. The IPA market was very closely guarded and those in the market made sure that they kept their near monopoly position. Maybe that's a contributory reason for the export market collapse after around 1840.

So here finally, on the following page, is recipe 2 converted to modern quantities and given some interpretation to render it suitable for a modern kitchen.

RECIPE 3 (HISTORICAL)

SHROPSHIRE PALE ALE

Domestic Brewing *1839*

ORIGINAL GRAVITY   NOT RECORDED

WATER   No analysis. Hard well water.

	25 LITRES	23 LITRES	5 UK GALS	5 US GALS
Pale Malt	5.5 kg	5.0 kg	11.1 lb	9 lb

START OF BOIL

Goldings 5% alpha-acid

	168 g	154 g	5.5 oz	4.5 oz

DRY HOP (CASK)

	0.5 litre	0.46 litre	1 pint	0.8 pint

BREWING METHOD

- Mash 1 kg (2 lb) at a time using as much water at the usual temperature as is needed to wet goods. (45–55°C)
- When thoroughly wetted, pour on 9 litres (2 gallons) of boiling water. Rest 3 hours.
- Run off the hot liquor onto the hops already in the cooler. Pour back on 6 litres (1½ gallons) boiling water. Rest 1 hour. Run off.
- Pour on 5 litres (1 gallon) boiling water. Run off. You should have around 23 litres (5 gallons) of wort.
- Boil 1 hour.
- Strain through hair sieves into coolers.
- When cool, start yeast and leave overnight in 4 litres (1 gallon) of wort.
- Add the rest of the liquor in 12 hour intervals over the next day.
- Stand 8–10 days.
- Rack into new keg.
- Add ½ litre (1 pint) of hot hops which have been infused in boiling water.
- Close down the keg.

RACKING GRAVITY   Not recorded

ALCOHOL CONTENT   Not recorded

BITTERNESS: 67 EBU

COLOUR: 4.0 EBC

COMMENTS   This country ale has included so many practices, which we no longer know about, never mind actually apply them. It is here for fun, for IPA enthusiasts who want to get back just that one step further than the industrialised ale brewing of the nineteenth century.

Eccentric Thoughts

Herbert James wrote on India Pale Ale at length between 1864-1872. I studied his fifth edition. He stated without any embarrassment that his rules on brewing are strictly practical and he pays no attention to the theory of the chemistry. He did have an opinion on virtually everything, including strike temperatures. He kept his strike temperature in winter at around 76.7°C (170°F) but lowered it to 73.9°C (165°F) in summer. What we don't know is what temperature the mash settled out at, but after shooting in the goods and stirring well, he then ran in the same amount of water again at 85°C–90.6°C (185–195°F), "to raise the temperature". To this second addition was added, "over or under the goods". By this was meant that the water was often run in the top but frequently forced up from underneath the mash. This helped carry fine grist to the surface which assisted running the wort off and also helped stir the mash.

We would imagine this to have again been a very hot mash.

The goods were then rested two hours, the first wort run off and the goods then sparged. Like his mentor Levesque, James was a sparger by the middle of the century. Levesque however mashed at around 62–64°C (143–148°F), which we now consider to be on the cool side. As was common at the time, his second mashes were around 6°C (10–12°F) warmer than his first.

Mash temperatures remain an intractable problem for brewers wishing to recreate authentic beers. We know with certainty that the amylase enzymes, responsible for converting starch into fermentable sugar, are largely destroyed above 70°C (158°F). However, not all enzyme molecules will cease to work immediately. Some conversion will take place even at the higher temperatures being recommended but at these high temperatures a lot of starch will only be converted into higher sugars instead of maltose and these larger sugar molecules may or may not ferment easily, or not at all or only after a very long time. IPA by definition will be given a very long time to mature, and by the time the beer reached its destination, maybe even these higher sugars had been converted into alcohol and the beer finished. We don't know. It is in fact up to the modern day brewer or brewster to make their own decision. There is nothing wrong with playing Vivaldi on a modern instrument, but many prefer to hear an original instrument and put up with the idiosyncrasies. My own opinion is, that commercial brewers can't afford inefficient mashes and fermentations. We, as home-brewers, can, and I think we should enjoy that liberty. Hence I love idiosyncratic brewing.

So if we think boiling is boiling, and sparging is sparging then life can be full of surprises. If boiling without the hops is quaint, try some of the following thoughts on Victorian Pale and India Pale Ales. Don't ask me to make up your mind. Courage!

Levesque (1854) provides us with no less than five methods of boiling a pale or India Ale. Worthy of note is that he boiled very short to "preserve flavours", never more than one hour for a first wort and $1\frac{1}{2}$ hours for the second. Of course he probably didn't mix the worts when making an IPA as he would have been looking for a starting gravity up around 1070. If his boiler was big enough he would have mixed the worts to make a pale ale. Certainly the third wort was used for a table beer or was used as liquor for a mash the next day. He certainly didn't sparge.

Of Levesque's five methods of boiling, the second comes closest to our present day method. He boiled the wort 40 minutes, then added hops and boiled until separation of farinaceous particles occurred, which he reckoned should not exceed an additional fifteen minutes. Hence the bittering components, the alpha acids only received fifteen minutes for isomerisation to occur, which is definitely the bottom end of sufficient. Again he was mindful of preserving the hop aroma and this requires a short hop boil to avoid steam distilling out the oils, but it must be remembered that if the hops were boiled for less than twenty minutes he won't have realised their full bittering potential.

I include his next method for the novelty. If anyone actually tries it, they should let me know how it worked, if they are still alive. This third method involved boiling until the hot break and then discharging everything from the boiler, including the hops into the cask, and bunging down. A safety valve was fitted and the liquor left untouched to "ferment and depurate without any addition of yeast, which will require 12 months for ordinary ale". I reached for my hard hat and then read on. Levesque argued that the vacuum caused by the wort cooling would furnish room for the carbon dioxide formed during fermentation.

"The fermentation and depuration takes eighteen months to two years for a 45 gravity ale in a temperate cellar" he writes. Now we are all wondering where the yeast comes from in order for any fermentation to take place. We generally imagine that a one-hour boil would put any micro-organism such as yeast, firmly to the sword. Of course, yeast belongs to the fungi, which are some of the world's great survivors. Certainly only very few yeast cells could survive such treatment and presumably they were sufficient to ferment the maltose. There can have been virtually no residual oxygen in the wort, straight after boiling and so it would be impossible for any aerobic fermentation to take place. This means that the yeast cells which are available would have no chance of reproducing without oxygen.

It is worth noting at this point that by the end of the nineteenth century, beer brewing authorities were no longer forming an orderly queue to rubbish Levesque. Everyone was having a pop at him. This third method of boiling may explain why.

However, little happens in history without reason and as the IPAs were to endure a long sea journey anyway, there seemed little reason to worry over a long fermentation, not even as long as twelve months. We are assured that "this technique may take 18 months to 2 years for stronger ales and lends itself to long journeys". So anyone wanting to brew an authentic IPA may not be able to avoid some adventuresome brews!

Koranzas points out that despite the scalding and working with hot tar, casks still managed to harbour some microbes and he assumes that Brettanomyces would have lingered in the wood and imparted a "horsey" character as he puts it. Brettanomyces is similar to the yeast used in some of the modern day Lambics and they have a distinctive sour flavour. I have already indicated that I think the "intentional" creation of some of these flavours has more to do with the brewer's inability to get on top of hygiene problems and they are not to my taste, but nineteenth century literature seems to imply that they may have been sought after and thus may well have found resonance in foreign parts inhabited by homesick colonials. I doubt that sour beers were part of the IPA culture and enough IPA arrived in India in a quite spoiled state without IPA brewers building spoilage by idiosyncrasy.

Despite the eccentricity of method number three (which I report without much hope of anyone trying it), his fourth method was commonly in use among cottage brewers and may have had an impact on pale ale. It is certainly mentioned in several housebrew sources. He boiled the wort without the hops for 30–45 minutes, having previously rubbed the intended amount of hops with the hands and deposited them in the cask in which his liquor was intended to remain. This rubbing process is probably quite pointless when copper hopping but may serve a purpose of breaking open the lupulin sacks, which may otherwise be able to remain intact when the flowers are not subjected to being banged around for an hour in a boiling wort.

He then turned the boiling wort into the cask and when full to the bung fixed the safety valve. This last step was not common. Most cooled first to around 30°C (86°F) and then added yeast.

The use of coolers was not universal and so many beers may have retained a residual haze of unprecipitated protein material, but this was not considered a problem until fairly recently. Do remember that we cannot compare our brew lengths of five to ten gallons with the monster brews commonly put on in the nineteenth century. If a sizeable brew was set on, then it would take a good time for the wort to cool and so the question is, does only a boil cause isomerisation of non-bittering components to the bittering alpha acids or does it already occur in temperatures close to boiling? If the latter is true then some bittering may have occurred.

Levesque seems to be completely confused with regard to the yeast, so much so that I wonder if he considered pitching the yeast at the right temperature as self evident. But I don't think so! He continues, "It may be inconvenient to adopt this method of boiling a considerable quantity together; but in the smaller, moveable bodies, there can be no objection, if the time of keeping is not an object. This process will suit the nobleman or private gentleman, where expense is not spared to procure that exhilarating old English luxury of superlative quality." The question remains again, how authentic do we want to be?

His fifth and final method finds much favour in many country recipes. "Boil but a small quantity of hops with the worts to the amount of one fourth part, or in fact, any quantity the brewer's judgement may dictate; and reserve the remainder to be put in the vat at the time of racking and storing the beer."

He rails against steeping hops prior to boiling although this too was common. He said "If more flavour is required, dry hop".

Herbert James seems to have been president of the Levesque fan club. Not an easy banner to carry! He considered an export ale should have a gravity of 1072 to 1083 but for domestic use he settled at 1064. Taking the export ales, he expected to get three barrels from each quarter mashed which in our modern domestic house brewery would yield us 19 litres from 5.4 kg of very pale malt.

RECIPE 4 (HISTORICAL)

HERBERT JAMES' 23 LB INDIA ALE (1864)

James gives us a variety of OG values, boiling times and hopping rates for an India Ale. He despised scientific theory and this may account for his haphazard amounts. I include his recipes, because at the time his hostile attitude to biochemistry was very common. 23 lb was a reference to the original gravity.

ORIGINAL GRAVITY 1072 18° PLATO

WATER No analysis. Hard well water.

	25 LITRES	23 LITRES	5 UK GALS	5 US GALS
Pale Malt	7.1 kg	6.5 kg	14.4 lb	11.6 lb

END OF BOIL

Goldings 5% alpha-acid.

	220-265 g	200-245 g	7.5-9 oz	6-7.2 oz

DRY HOP (CASK)

Never steep copper hops before boiling, but instead, if more flavour needed, dry hop. No quantities given.

BREWING METHOD

- Set on a stiff mash by wetting the goods with water at 77–79°C (170–175 °F) by over or under turning (bottom or top mashing).
- Then turn on 5 litres (1gal) at 85–88°C (185–190°F) to raise temperature to the mash temperature of 65°C (149°F).
- Stand 2 hours.
- The tap temperature should be 61–64°C (142–146°F).
- Run off wort.
- Boil for 5–6 hours
- Run off the hot wort onto the hops.
- Cool, pitch the yeast and attenuate very low, so that the beer goes in the keg or bottle nearly flat.
- Ferment at 14°C (58°F) in October or 10°C (50°F) in March, in deference to ambient temperatures.

RACKING GRAVITY

No figures given but the advice was given, "leave less saccharine in the beer but infuse more hops, to decrease the risk of explosion".

ALCOHOL CONTENT: 7.7% V/V   6.6% W/W

COLOUR: 4.0 EBC

COMMENTS   A second mash was done 7°C (10–12°F) above the first mash. I doubt if the worts were combined if a 1072 ale were to be achieved. Mixing the worts must be done judiciously although if the 5–6 hour boil is carried out, there is little chance of ending up with a wort that is too thin. Such long boils not only evaporated water from the wort but materially altered the solubility of the hot break in the liquor. Sambrook and I (*Historical Companion*) have both commented at length on this English quirk.

The long boil of five to six hours was by no means uncommon, although I believe that generally economic demands required more brevity. Such a long boil does substantially alter the nature of the beer. Much material such as sticky water insoluble proteins are precipitated out during the boil. The swirling action of the boil causes the tiny suspended particles to collide and coagulate. When large enough they settle out. This is called the hot break and usually occurs after around 60 minutes boiling. The extended boil way beyond one hour, causes some of the particles to break down and form molecules small enough to dissolve in the wort. One achieves a very nutritious beer this way. Many Continental brewers greatly admired this technique of long boiling and maturing. They asked how British brewers managed to use so much fuel and tie up so much capital and still stay in business!

If so called "30 lb Ales" were to be made (SG. 1083) they were boiled for two hours. The description 30 lb Ale refers to the then common method of measuring gravity. 30 lb described the amount of sugar (fermentable material) which would need to be added to one barrel of water (usually 36 gallons by the 1840s) in order to produce the same hydrometer reading as the wort. This was useful in the years before hydrometers were available. A gallon of wort was weighed and allowing for the weight of one gallon of water, beer worts could be compared. When hydrometers arrived they were initially calibrated directly in pounds of sugar per barrel. One can still buy home-brew and home-winemaking hydrometers marked in lb per gallon.

James gives us a variety of original gravities for an India Ale but there are also principle differences in the boiling times and hop amounts. There doesn't seem to be any particular pattern to his choice of method.

RECIPE 5

HERBERT JAMES' 30 LB INDIA PALE ALE (1864)

ORIGINAL GRAVITY		1083	21° PLATO	

WATER   No analysis. Hard well water

	25 LITRES	23 LITRES	5 UK GALS	5 US GALS
Pale Malt	8.5 kg	7.8 kg	17.2 lb	14.0 lb

END OF BOIL

Goldings 5% alpha-acid.

	424 g	390 g	14 oz	11.5 oz

DRY HOP (CASK)

Never steep copper hops before boiling, but instead, if more flavour is needed, dry hop. No quantities given.

BREWING METHOD

- Set on a stiff mash by wetting the goods with water at 77–79°C (170–175 °F) by over or under turning (bottom or top mashing).
- Then turn on 5 litres (1 gallon) at 85–88 °C (185–190°F) to raise temperature to the mash temperature of 65°C (149°F).
- Stand 2 hours.
- The tap temperature should be 61–64°C (142–146°F).
- Run off wort.
- Boil for 2 hours
- Run off the hot wort onto the hops.
- Cool, pitch the yeast and attenuate very low, so that the beer goes in the keg or bottle nearly flat.
- Ferment at 14°C (58°F) in October or 10°C (50°F) in March, in deference to ambient temperatures.
- Mature for at least one year.

RACKING GRAVITY

No figures given but "leave less saccharine in the beer but infuse more hops, to decrease the risk of explosion".

ALCOHOL CONTENT	9.9% v/v	7.4% w/w

BITTERNESS   170 EBU but not relevant

COLOUR   4.0 EBC

COMMENTS   This was mashed twice in the normal way, the second mash being run at about 10°C hotter than the first. The second wort was used to bring the first wort to the right gravity and the remainder used for a second weaker beer, maybe a mild ale.

I have already intimated that brewing a genuine IPA will require many home brewers to rethink their technique. Some Burton Brewers used a slow boil over three hours "to prevent rank bitterness and removal of aromatic material." I suspect a trade secret was being protected here for the slow boil was surely to keep the beer really pale and prevent any darkening at all. Dr. John Harrison of Durden Park suspects that the plant in Burton Breweries was simply not up to maintaining a decent boil. I'm not sure where the "rank bitterness" should come from, but it is true that aromatic material is best kept in by a slow boil with the lid on. Interestingly enough most modern home brewers think there is merit in a fast boil with the lid off. The lid is removed to prevent "rank bitterness" from some unspecified hop oils which need steam distilling off and the boil vigorous in order to assist coagulation of the suspended particles and cause the hot break to occur properly.

I have always preferred a slightly slower, partial-lid-on boil, in order to keep the time required to bring the liquor to the boil and the energy required to maintain the boil to a minimum. I also live in a relatively temperate and damp part of the world and we don't win praise round here for filling the brewhouse with steam. It takes days to ventilate, with the attendant risk of black moulds growing on any rough surface. And the fact that I could claim the pedigree of nineteenth-century Burton Brewers always seemed justification enough. I do have to take a fair amount of flack from modern craft brewers, but then "Ask ten brewers and you'll get eleven opinions" is the saying, and sometimes one simply has to adjust to what is practical. That attitude definitely has historical precedence.

The amount of hops chosen for the 1083 Ale is enormous. Of course we know little about the bittering properties of Pale East Kent Hops. We assume they were not as rich in alpha-acids as present day crops, but nevertheless, 16 lb per quarter (390g per 23 litres or 5 imperial gallons) is astounding. 10–12 lb per quarter were used if the ale was only to keep one year. In this recipe the hot wort is run onto the hops, which may have isomerised less bittering material than boiling the hops with the wort. However, as James brewed on something like fifty times the scale that we can manage, the wort must have remained hot long enough to produce considerable bittering. We don't know if he left the hops in the fermentation, as was sometimes done, or, more likely, pressed them out before pitching the yeast. Both were common practice and I would assume that if he didn't boil the hops in the wort, he only removed them before kegging. In my experience, not filtering off the hops after the boil, but leaving the flowers in for the fermentation certainly produces a different beer with exceptionally powerful bittering.

It appears that the hop amounts chosen depended more on the need to keep the beer a considerable time, than on taste alone. Hops do help preserve a beer and one can get used to very bitter beers. In fact if one is used to such enormous hop quantities in beer, then an ale which has been "normally hopped" will taste quite bland. This explains James' recipe for a domestic IPA. Soldiers and civil servants returning from the former Colonies, quite missed their regular brew and so there was demand for IPA at home. This was always brewed less strongly and with more regular amounts of hops. It never tasted the same as a beer which has spent many months on board a violently swaying ship in tropical heat. Any brewer in serious business was not going to tie up capital and equipment for years if he didn't have to. This was especially important when selling against competition which was not producing such a noble product. It was inevitable that drinkers compared the price of their beloved IPA, which they remembered so fondly from the days full of adventure in the Indies, with the competitor's product next to it on the bar. It was probably impossible to maintain the IPA standards under these circumstances.

James also instructs us to "attenuate very low". Many other writers report that they leave IPA export bitters with less saccharine in the young beer than normal but infuse more hops to help keeping and reduce explosion risk. So flat casking seems to have been common practice.

Fermentation takes place in several distinct phases. The first phase is the lag, during which time the yeast uses oxygen in order to reproduce and form a yeast cell colony capable of fermenting so much sugar. Brewers lucky enough to be able to get working yeast directly from a brewery may hardly notice the lag time as a good working yeast can take off in a few hours.

Then comes the time of high activity, called the primary fermentation. Normally the primary fermentation is considered finished when the fermenting young beer no longer builds a stable head. This begins to occur around 1040 because as the beer density goes down during fermentation, the solids are less able to float but the exact point will depend on the yeast, the temperature and maybe even the original gravity. The strong fermentation begins to wind down as more fermentable material is used up. In order to give a beer its head when served, brewers transfer the beer into casks before the primary fermentation has completely ceased. Domestic Ales were fermented according to the maxim, "ferment all keeping beers to one quarter of their starting gravity". Levesque was more circumspect and relied on the stricter maxim, "ferment all beers to one quarter of starting gravity, not exceeding 70". This gives us a maximum casking gravity of 1017.

By a "keeping beer" (which IPAs certainly were), we may understand an original gravity of at least 1060. This means the beer was transferred at around 1015 and the pressure in the barrel must have been enormous. Provided the beer is kept cool and the barrel filled to capacity, this obviously wasn't too much of a problem. Before shipping an IPA however, the pressure was released, to prevent barrels bursting as the temperature rose. The constant agitation during the journey was also likely to cause the gas to come out of solution and increase the pressure on the barrel, hence the need to fill casks to capacity.

A good amount of dissolved carbon dioxide was considered no bad thing in a domestic beer as it allowed the maturation time to be kept to a minimum. A good head was a certainty if you kegged at 1015 to 1017, but using the primary fermentation sugar to create a head may not be done with a beer, which is to be shaken and kept warm for a long time. This combination allows a healthy secondary fermentation to take place, during which the yeast breaks down heavier molecules and continues to produce carbon dioxide gas. Unless the young beer is totally flat before the voyage commenced, the secondary fermentation may spring the container during shaking in tropical heat. "Attenuate very low" is an instruction not to fill the beer into barrels before the specific gravity is approaching 1010. As alcohol has a lower density than water, it is possible to get a specific gravity of less than 1000, although this is unlikely in any beer worth drinking because of the dissolved but non-fermentable material, which will make the gravity appear higher than it would be if one considered fermentable material alone.

Burton upon Trent

So far we have skirted round what became the home of IPA brewing, Burton upon Trent. It was always supposed that the high gypsum content of Burton water, was responsible for the excellent beers brewed there. I'm not going to try and fly in the face of popular belief, but there is always more than one factor affecting any empirical observation or hypothesis. The fact is, that although Burton water is good for beer, it doesn't have to be Burton water in order to make a superb IPA, as the Amsinck recipes will illustrate, but in deference to Burton and its pivotal place in brewing history, we ought to look at a few brews from that place. Firstly then a wacky one.

RECIPE 6

Burton Pale Ale. Domestic Brewer *1839*

BURTON IPA 1839

ORIGINAL GRAVITY   1083   21° PLATO

WATER   No analysis. Gypsum saturated

	25 LITRES	23 LITRES	5 UK GALS	5 US GALS
Pale (as straw) Malt				
	10.6 kg	9.8 kg	21.5 lb	17.4 lb

START OF BOIL

Goldings 5% alpha-acid.				
	200 g	183 g	6.7 oz	5.4 oz

BREWING METHOD

- Use only the palest malt. The beer must be as pale as straw.
- Only use gypsum rich water.
- Heat the water to 74–76°C (165–170°F).
- Mash for 1 hour.
- Rest for 1 hour while the liquor infuses.
- Run off the first wort.
- Infuse a second time for 2 hours with water at 85°C (185°F).
- Add pale hops and boil.
- Add 1 teaspoon of honey 15 minutes before the end of the boil.
- Cool, and strain off the hops before pitching the yeast.

First mash: 1 hour at 66°C (151°F). Rest for 1 hour. Run off first wort.
Second mash: Infuse for 2 hours at 80°C (176°F). Run of second wort
and combine it with the first to give a gravity of around 1070.

BOIL TIME   Boil the wort and hops for $2\frac{1}{2}$ hours. Add 1 tea
spoon of honey 15 minutes before the end of the boil.

FERMENTATION   Ferment at 18°C (65°F)

RACKING GRAVITY   Not given

ALCOHOL CONTENT	9.9% v/v	7.4% w/w

BITTERNESS   80 EBU

COLOUR   4.0 EBC

COMMENTS   This recipe is low on detail, which is a sign that the writer considered it such a common method that brewers of the day would have immediately recognised what they had to do. We can obviously use any mashing technique which best suits us. The Burton breweries did the same, in as much as they worked to the best advantage of their brewing system.

The addition of honey was not usual, and this brewer promised himself better keeping properties by the use of honey.

Once again we are confronted by the shift in the meaning of the word "mash". This beer was mashed one hour and infused one hour. It was also a mighty brew for a domestic recipe, the original calling for ten quarters of malt which is nearly one and a half metric tonnes. Thus the instruction "mash for one hour" meant that the poor assistant paddled in the thick heavy porridge with his mashing oar for a full hour, in order to get the heat evenly distributed. This too must have affected the quality and nature of the beer. Such long turning leads to aerial oxidation and a darkening of the beer. Most home-brewers nowadays probably mash for five or ten minutes and then infuse for ninety minutes.

Many additives were used in this brew such as Jalap, (a purgative root of a South American ivy), sal prunela (a nitrate used to treat throat infections) etc. to keep the yeast working. This would not be necessary with modern day yeasts and mashed worts and our quest for the genuine article need not lead us to use such awful substances.

Honey was supposed to prevent secondary fermentation, a fore-runner it was believed, to acidity forming. This is almost certainly a misconception but if you like honey beers, why not? This assertion seems to be unique to this brew and I can find no scientific justification for believing honey has preservative properties. The amounts used could hardly have influenced the taste.

This recipe does however stand in stark contrast to the story that Burton brewers had sworn an oath that they used nothing in their beers but malt, hops, water and yeast. No one it seems believed them at the time, (several writers derided the notion) but to declare the intention was obviously considered the nobler thing to do. We should persevere with this sentiment, even though our notion of IPA as the pure beverage of the Empire keeps taking a hammering.

Burton and Gypsum

The word Burton can't be dropped in brewing circles without the listeners thinking "Ah! The best brewing water in the world." Listen carefully and you'll hear another myth bite the dust. The Burton water myth was also prevalent in the nineteenth century when IPA had its birth. Most writers of that time praised the brewing qualities of the water from that area, the calcium and sulphate ion concentrations attracting most attention. The fact is that there were seven wells in use in Burton on Trent around 1840, but only two were used for providing brewing water on a *regular* basis. This means however that any one of the seven *may* have provided water for any odd brew. The analysis sheets of three of them, which did provide brewing water at one time or another, make interesting reading. James reproduced them to make this very point.

Burton upon Trent Brewing Wells Analysis (James 1864)

Salt grains in Imperial gallons (mg/l)	Well 1		Well 2		Well 3	
Calcium sulphate	71	(88)	25.5	(30)	7	(9)
Calcium hydrogen carbonate	9	(11)	18	(22)	16	(20)
Magnesium carbonate	6	(7.5)	9	(11)	2	(2.5)
Magnesium sulphate	12	(15)	0		0	
Sodium sulphate	13	(16)	8	(10)	4	(5)
Sodium chloride	9	(11)	10	(12)	7	(8.6)
Potassium chloride	1	(1.2)	2	(2.4)	13	(16)
Magnesium chloride	0		0		7	(9)
Carbonate of protoxide of iron	1.2	(1.5)	0.9	(1)	Trace	

The only remarkable thing is how constant virtually every thing is *apart* from the calcium sulphate concentration. The only thing which isn't a common factor is the gypsum row! And yet brewers praise the gypsum as being the be-all and end-all of brewing water. Unfortunately we don't know if the IPAs from Well 3 were inferior.

The only Victorian writer who consistently provides a brewing-water analysis table (if at all possible) is Amsinck and he reports categorically that the only important factor in making beer is the skill of the maltster and brewer and is derisive of the Burton factor. His recipes show that IPA was brewed with anything and he quotes the charming anecdote about rain water, which would be free of all salts:

"I brewed a pale ale from rain water in a small brewhouse. I sent three hogsheads of this ale to a brother in the artillery in Madras, asking for an honest report (no flummery). His report, as good as any ale that ever reached India. So much for sulphate of lime is indispensable."

His second story sounds equally unlikely, but probably also true.

"A pale ale has been pronounced equal, and identical in flavour, with the finest Burton, has been brewed from pond and surface water, the main supply from a duck pond, percolating through the earth, about 40 feet into a basin, three or four feet deep, and fed by no spring."

Maybe this explains the Victorian proverb, "You've got to eat a peck of dirt before you die."

The general opinion on the importance of water could be summarised with that most Victorian of expressions, "humbug". More modern data shows us the futility of trying to regulate water values by choosing a supply.

Water Supply Variation (during the day and during a decade).

	Public		*Well*	
ppm	*Day*	*Night*	*1975*	*1962*
pH	7.6	7.6	7.0	7.0
NO_3^-	5	36	18	28
SO_4^{2-}	27	32	16	31
HCO_3^-	87	100	820	848
Ca^{2+}	88	100	352	72
Mg^{2+}	21	14	24	72
Na^+	21	37	54	26

Brigg, Hough and Stevens. Brewing Science 1976

The public supply shows such a worrying nitrate and sodium ion variation that I shall only ever run off my brewing water from the mains during the day as nitrates are very detrimental to yeast health.

The well water changes with the years too. This explains why so many small scale brewers are making use of the Murphy treatment now available through Brupaks (Appendix 2).

Many more Burton India Pale Ale recipes follow.

Hops and History

Hops and Historical Recipes for English East India Pale Ales

How to choose the recipes to include is always a problem. I've decided to take only those which have something remarkable about them. This may be something quirky, but more likely it is because someone enthused particularly about the resulting beer.

I haven't been able to resist the inclusion of all the Amsinck East India Pale Ales. These span a time of at least thirty years, and are quite difficult to date exactly. He started recording them around 1830, although I took them from the final edition of his book, some thirty years later. Some were brewed by him, others by unknown brewers, whom he knew and admired, but rarely identified. This was such common practice in Victorian times that I suspect there must have been a permanent fear of litigation if something went wrong. We only have to refer to the novels of Charles Dickens to know what that meant.

I think the Amsinck records form an excellent cross section of IPA brewing during the key time of colonial expansion. He was very thorough in his record keeping and gives considerable detail about the type of brewery and equipment he thought best. That done, he doesn't include details of where the actual breweries he reported on were, or the year the gyle was brewed, or if his "best practice," brew houses were actually used. Shame!

I have adhered to Amsinck's original recipes as closely as my own knowledge of Victorian brewing will allow. It is up to you to decide when things seem too over-the-top for our modern ideas.

The hop quantities he gives are anything up to five times that which some other contemporaries utilised, but he was by no means alone in using such huge amounts. I was worried by this and in the past have had to put up with vitriolic letters from home brewers pointing out how ridiculous this is and how stupid I am to propagate such folly. Well, history is history and I cannot change it to suit modern notions. I don't believe it was folly either and the modern day attitude to hop quantities was also around 150 years ago. We know this to be so because this attitude was exactly the parsimony that Amsinck himself railed against. It seems that times never really change. "Once brewers put pockets of hops in, now they add them to suit their pockets", seems to have been his cry.

The argument the doubters use is that you can only get so much hop oil and alpha-acid into a solution, and the rest is wasted. I generally accept the argument as scientifically sound, but when tested it does not seem to hold. Adding huge amounts of hops does alter the beer. There may be a ceiling level for bittering, but I've never reached it. However, the bittering compounds mellow with time. Drink an IPA that is a fortnight old and you will choke on the hops. Drink the same beer a year later and the alpha-acids have changed again into a whole new spectrum of flavours. This means we can't ruin a beer with bittering compounds, provided we are prepared to let it mature properly, but hops are not only about bittering. They continue to influence beer long after any bittering ceiling, if such a thing exists, has been reached. Whenever I drink James McCrorie's incredible historic India Ales he brews for Durden Park, and I ask him his secret, he says, "Three things Clive, hops, hops and then more hops." He also regulates the Original Gravity by parsimonious sparging. Historically, brewers sparged the full volume only to make a second weaker beer, which is a piece of good housekeeping with which most craft brewers have dispensed.

But to finish with hops! There is little point in giving a bittering figure in EBU for the recipes which require huge quantities. I have just established that they have to be kept until the initial bittering compounds have altered into taste components more in tune with our palates. Hence we can only give a hypothetical EBU figure for when they were made, not when they are drunk. So why have I bothered to give a figure? It is still useful to be able to relate IPA hopping rates to our modern practice. Incidentally, James's modern pale ale, to his own recipe, has been 'Showcased' at the Beauty of Hops competition in an effort to show modern commercial brewers what they could achieve if they tried. One retired Head Brewer (of a major national brewery) commented "I wish I had been allowed to brew a beer as good as this during my career". Over 1,000 lucky visitors to the Great British Beer Festival have been able to sample this beer over the past few years. The recipe follows later.

The original hop types are no longer available in the form that they were used in the nineteenth century. I am sure all the Amsinck recipes used Goldings, around 4.5% alpha-acid. But here is another problem. UK East Kent Goldings in 1996 were 4.5% alpha-acid. The 1999 crop was assayed at 6.6%. The next harvest may be lower again, or even a little higher. Furthermore, we always make the assumption that present day hops have a more intense effect on beer than they could have had 150 years ago. This is a huge guess for which there is absolutely no evidence. It is a convenient argument, because it infers that putting in a fifth as much nowadays is having the same effect as adding five times the amount a century and a half ago. The convenience is in the fact that hops are the most expensive ingredient and hop parsimony is not only sound economics but is also made to appear to be a historically accurate step. In other words, we are doing it right by ignoring the Victorian recipes. It's rubbish of course! Brewers have always tried to get away with cheap solutions, and the beauty of home brewing is that we don't have to follow suit.

Some knowledgeable brewers and horticulturists have argued, that over the years our hop stock is likely to have degenerated and be less powerful in flavouring. The truth is, we have no way of knowing what Victorian hops were like. We may hanker after authentic brews, but when the original IPAs were being brewed, no one was afraid to take that which was to hand so we cannot be sure about anything. This is certainly why I am able to include an original nineteenth century IPA brewed with Bavarian hops, which were, at the time, cheaper than the best Kent or Farnham varieties and generally supposed to be no way as good as the popular English varieties. And then again, maybe Bavarian were sometimes used out of conviction, not economic convenience.

Some general points of information must be born in mind when trying Amsinck brews. Amsinck always used at least two mashes. He rarely used the same ratio of mash water for different brews. I therefore have given his first to second mash ratio. Suppose the ratio of liquor used in each mash is 3:1. This means a brew of length 25 litres had a first mash of about 17 litres, the wort was run off and then it was remashed with a second mash of 8 litres, or in gallons, first mash 3.3 gallons and second mash 1.6 gallons. He didn't sparge out of conviction. Recipes which include a sparge, are probably of Scottish origin; maybe even brewed by a visiting Scottish brewer.

A word on racking gravity. These beers were either racked flat, or often as not, racked as normal for a beer, and then shortly before the journey, the pressure was released. Hence, the racking gravities given in the recipes do not allow for the long sea voyage. A lot will go on in a bottle in a year. If you use bottles, always release the pressure shortly after racking. A judicious approach is needed too if kegging the IPA, although modern kegs have a pressure release system.

My only reservation about Amsinck is that he may have acted as censor and rejected other people's work on a whim or downright prejudice. I personally don't think he is guilty of this but it is a risk we take when delving into history and such problems should form the subject of further research.

Many beers were named according to the price they fetched per barrel. As I'm actually old enough to remember L.s.d, I'd better elucidate. The L stood for pounds sterling and has over the years shifted its design to the current £ sign. The s. was shillings, of which there were twenty to a pound and the d. was pence of which there were twelve to a shilling. Shillings were not often abbreviated in shop windows with an s. unless they occurred with a £ sign or L e.g. £3.10s. If shillings appeared on their own, as would happen with ten shillings and sixpence, it was more common to write it as 10/6. This was pronounced "ten and six". 10/- thus meant ten shillings and no pence. If no pence were involved in a price, it was common to express prices larger than one pound, in shillings. A 60/- Ale was a beer which sold for sixty shillings per barrel, which is the same as three pounds. If the shilling and pound signs were not available to printers they used an L instead of £ and so we often come across a sixty shilling ale as L3.

Non-British readers are by now convinced I'm mad and my exposition on L.s.d has probably ruined the credibility of this whole book. Nevertheless, it is all true! Horses, unlike beer, were, and probably still are sold in guineas and one guinea was a gold coin worth exactly 21/-. Be glad you purchased a book on IPA and not stud farming.

Specific gravity conversions into degrees Plato (°P) and percentage alcohol as volume of alcohol per volume of water (v/v), and weight of alcohol per weight of water (w/w), have been taken from Noonan's *New Brewing Lager Beers*. Such conversions are never entirely accurate unless the brewer knows how much of the measured gravity is fermentable material. This has to be assessed every brew and is known as the attenuation. Hence, the values given for percentages alcohol in the following recipes are only approximations.

Recipe Section

Recipes 7 to 17 follow in this section.

RECIPE 7 (HISTORICAL)

No. 25 in Amsinck's log

BURTON EAST INDIA PALE ALE 60/-

Amsinck moaned, "This gyle was brewed at Burton in olden times, when the ales from that locality were perfect in every sense. The large quantity of hops meant that it was a bitter ale, now the quantity is what suits the pocket of the brewer."

We don't know what the olden times were, but before 1830 I'd guess. This gyle was brewed in January.

ORIGINAL GRAVITY 1067		17° Plato	

WATER　　　Burton Well. No.3 analysis. Hard.

	25 LITRES	**23 LITRES**	**5 UK GALS**	**5 US GALS**
New Burton White Malt				
	6.3　kg	5.8　kg	12.8　lb	10.4　lb

START OF BOIL

East and Mid Kent (Goldings) 4.5% alpha-acid				
	440　g	405　g	14.8　oz	12.0　oz

BREWING METHOD

Boil the water overnight and allow it to cool. Infusion mash. Run off 1st wort and mash a 2nd time. No sparge. First to second mash ratio 1:1.

First mash: Strike 74°C (165°F) Mashed then rested 120 minutes. Settled at 66°C (150°F)

Second mash: Strike 82°C (180°F) Mash rested 60 minutes. Settled at 74°C (165°F)

BOIL TIME　　　120 minutes for both worts. Second wort turned onto first wort hops. Worts then combined.

FERMENTATION　　Pitched at 18°C (64°F). Cleansed after 16 hours when at 22°C (72°F). Racked after 4 days.

DRY HOPS (CASK)

	100　g	90　g	3.3　oz	2.7　oz

RACKING GRAVITY　　Racked after 4 days at 1031 (8°　Plato).

ALCOHOL CONTENT	8.7% v/v	6.9% w/w

BITTERNESS   159 EBU. Probably not relevant.

COLOUR   2.5 EBC

COMMENTS   The hop quantities are so extreme that I spent a long time convincing myself that I hadn't miscalculated. Amsinck insisted time and again that a proper IPA utilised such quantities.

This brew asks for white malt (see Appendix 3). Even though it was racked at 1031 the pressure may well have been released prior to shipping.

RECIPE 8 (HISTORICAL)

No. 26 in Amsinck's log

(NOT BURTON) EAST INDIA PALE ALE 60/- PER BARREL

Amsinck had given up Burton by now as a bad job and was pleased to brew elsewhere. He declared this brew "equal to any from Burton." This was brewed in a closed domed copper, "with the manhole shut and wasted through steam pipes into the pan". This seems to have been done to spite Burton Brewers, who used open slow boils for fear of colour or due to inefficient boilers. Brewed in March.

ORIGINAL GRAVITY 1065   16° Plato

WATER   No analysis. Hard

	25 LITRES	23 LITRES	5 UK GALS	5 US GALS
New Newark Pale				
	6.5 kg	5.9 kg	13.1 lb	10.6 lb

START OF BOIL

Choice East and Mid Kent. Goldings high aroma 4.5% alpha-acid

450 g	410 g	15 oz	12 oz

BREWING METHOD

Boil the liquor overnight and allow to cool. Infusion Mash. Two mashes and then sparged at 71°C (160°F), but the sparge was used as liquor for first the mash of a X ale the following day. First to second mash ratio 1:1.4

First mash: Strike 74°C (165°F) Mashed then stood 120 minutes. Settled at 64°C (149°F)

Second mash: Strike 82°C (180°F) Mash stood 60 minutes. Settled at 72°C (162°F)

BOIL TIME   90 minutes for both worts then combined just prior to kegging.

DRY HOP (CASK)

90 g	85 g	3.1 oz	2.5 oz

FERMENTATION   Worts fermented separately. Pitched at 17°C (62°F). Rose to 22°C (72°F) during following 36 hours when cleansed. Kegged after 4 days.

RACKING GRAVITY   Kegged after 4 days at 1030 (7° Plato)

ALCOHOL CONTENT	8.6% v/v	6.8% w/w

BITTERNESS   162 EBU. Probably not relevant.

COLOUR   2.5 EBC

COMMENTS   If it breaks your heart to throw in such hop amounts, then try the Victorian ploy of using the same hops to flavour the table beer, which would have been made from the third washing.

When I tried to recreate a similar gyle to this, I extracted far more than expected and ended up adding this amount of hops to around 6½ gallons.

Victorian brewers roused their fermentations and this would be standard practice here too, although it is not mentioned in Amsinck's record. I recommend frequently aerating with sterile air.

JMcC comments, "Note the Sparging in his recipe and the use of the term 'cleansed' – this is certainly a Scottish Brewer – although why a second mash escapes me!" Note the fermentation temperatures and time!!

RECIPE 9 (HISTORICAL)

No. 27 in Amsinck's log

EAST INDIA PALE ALE
60/- PER BARREL

Many IPAs were kept over a year before being considered for drinking. This one was brewed in December, and described as "a gyle in splendid condition and fit to deliver to the trade in February." The trade may have been an exporter and so this beer still had a long trip ahead of it.

Note the use of white malt, finished at 30°C (86°F), much lower than our modern Pale Malt. (See Appendix 3). The technique suggests the brewer was Scottish, or had learned his craft North of the Border.

ORIGINAL GRAVITY	1067		17° Plato	

WATER	Analysis 5. Hard.			

	25 LITRES	**23 LITRES**	**5 UK GALS**	**5 US GALS**
New Derby White				
	6.55 kg	6.0 kg	13.2 lb	10.7 lb

START OF BOIL

East and Mid Kent high aroma Goldings, 3.5% alpha-acid				
	390 g	360 g	13.2 oz	10.7 oz

BREWING METHOD

Liquor boiled overnight and allowed to cool. Infusion Mash. Two mashes and then sparged at 71°C (160°F), but this return wort was probably used for a Table Beer. First to second mash ratio 1:0.6

First mash: Strike 73°C (164°F) Mashed then stood 120 minutes. Settled at 64°C (149°F)

Second mash: Strike 82°C (180°F) Mash stood 90 minutes. Settled at 69°C (156°F)

BOIL TIME	90 minutes for both worts then combined.			

DRY HOP (CASK)

	90 g	85 g	3.1 oz	2.5 oz

FERMENTATION   Pitched at 16°C (61°F). Rose to 22°C (72°F) during following 36 hours. Cleansed and kegged.

RACKING GRAVITY   Cleansed after 36 hours and transferred to settling back at 1035 (9° Plato). After 8 hours settling it was kegged.

ALCOHOL CONTENT	8.3% v/v	6.5% w/w

BITTERNESS   110 EBU. Probably not relevant.

COLOUR   2.0 EBC

COMMENTS   In all the recipes so far, Amsinck mentions, "dry hops added, shived same day, porous spiles not required". To shive was to stopper with weak thin cask plugs, called spiles which functioned as a safety valve, and the spiles not being porous indicates that the young beer was well flat and not much carbon dioxide was to be expected.

Again the term "cleansing" occurs. This was a racking process which effectively decants off the young beer from the solids, which are precipitated during the fermentation. This is good practice in a beer which is to keep.

Skimming is the removal of froth contaminated with hop resins. Allowing the resins and foam to sink back into the beer has a profound effect on the nature of the bittering and may lead to harshness.

RECIPE 10 (HISTORICAL)

No. 28 in Amsinck's log

SOFT WATER EAST INDIA PALE ALE
60/- PER BARREL

Amsinck wrote, "This gyle was brewed by my instructor, the liquor being different, the plant strange etc., he did not get the length right, with the required gravity. Tap heat too high, however it turned out well, the principle bulk was shipped to Sydney."

So this one wasn't first rate. That's still no reason to retaliate with Fosters.

ORIGINAL GRAVITY	1067	17° Plato

WATER   Analysis 3. Soft.

	25 LITRES	23 LITRES	5 UK GALS	5 US GALS
New Suffolk Pale				
	6.6 kg	6.1 kg	13.3 lb	10.8 lb

START OF BOIL

New choice East and Mid Kent Goldings, 3.5% alpha-acid

	370 g	340 g	12.3 oz	10.0 oz

BREWING METHOD

Liquor boiled overnight with 16g (0.6oz) gypsum and allowed to cool. Infusion Mash. Two mashes and then sparged at 71°C (160°F), but this return wort was used in the first mash for a Porter brewed the next day. First to second mash ratio 2:1

First mash: Strike 73°C (165°F). Mashed and then stood 120 minutes. Settled at 66°C (151°F)

Second mash: Strike 81°C (178°F). Mashed and then stood 90 minutes. Settled at 71°C (160°F)

BOIL TIME   1st wort boiled 120 minutes, 2nd wort boiled 105 minutes before both worts were combined.

DRY HOP (CASK)

	90 g	85 g	3.1 oz	2.5 oz

FERMENTATION   Pitched at 16°C (61°F). Rose to 22°C (72°F) during following 36 hours.

RACKING GRAVITY   Cleansed after 36 hours and transferred into hogsheads at 1032 (8° Plato). After 1 week, run into settling back for 6 hours then dry hopped and kegged.

ALCOHOL CONTENT	8.3% v/v	6.5% w/w

BITTERNESS   133 EBU. Probably not relevant.

COLOUR   2.0 EBC

COMMENTS   This IPA is remarkable for the soft water used, this not usually being associated with ale brewing. Despite his frequently encountered "Who needs calcium sulphate in their water?" attitude, Amsinck admits to throwing 30 lb of Plaster of Paris into this brew liquor. It was brewed in March.

I am surprised he boiled soft water overnight as there was presumably little carbonate present to precipitate. Maybe it was force of habit. We can safely assume he wasn't the one who had to get the coal in!

RECIPE 11 (HISTORICAL)

No. 29 in Amsinck's log

BURTON EAST INDIA PALE ALE
60/- PER BARREL

This brewery was apparently famous for its splendid Pale and Strong Ales. All the more surprising that the brewer seems to have had no idea about the water he brewed with, nor do we know anything about the brewery. One can only assume, that famous brewers were invited along to do a guest brew, a tradition which still seems to exist judging by the annual coming together of great minds in the White Horse on Parson's Green. Again, with the wisdom of hindsight Amsinck would have used less hops.

This was a March brew and the sparging and cleansing led James Mc Crorie to believe it to have Scottish origins. I really can't forgive Amsinck his reluctance to tell us about the brewery and brewer.

ORIGINAL GRAVITY 1064	16° Plato

WATER   Analysis 9. Hard.

	25 LITRES	23 LITRES	5 UK GALS	5 US GALS
New Derby Pale				
	5.5 kg	5.0 kg	11.1 lb	9.0 lb

START OF BOIL

New choice East and Mid Kent high aroma 3.5% alpha-acid

	25 LITRES	23 LITRES	5 UK GALS	5 US GALS
	340 g	313 g	11.4 oz	9.3 oz
	(226 g)	(207 g)	(7.6 oz)	(6.1 oz)

BREWING METHOD

Liquor boiled overnight and allowed to cool. Three infusion mashes and a sparge at 71°C (160°F). 3rd mash and sparge used as return wort. Their use is not given. First to second mash ratio 3:1

First mash: Strike 73°C (164°F). Mashed and then stood 120 minutes. Settled at 65°C (149°F)

Second mash: Strike 88°C (190°F). Mashed and then stood 30 minutes. Settled at 73°C (164°F)

BOIL TIME   1st wort boiled 90 minutes, 2nd wort boiled 90 minutes and both worts then combined.

DRY HOP (CASK)

	25 LITRES	23 LITRES	5 UK GALS	5 US GALS
	90 g	114 g	4.1 oz	3.3 oz
	(81 g)	(74 g)	(2.7 oz)	(2.2 oz)

FERMENTATION   Pitched at 17°C (63°F). Rose to 23°C (73°F) during following 36 hours.

RACKING GRAVITY   Cleansed into butts after 36 hours at 1035 (9° Plato). After 4 days, transferred into kegs, dry hops added and closed.

ALCOHOL CONTENT   8.3% v/v   6.5% w/w

BITTERNESS   113 EBU (73 EBU). Probably not relevant.

COLOUR   3.0 EBC

COMMENTS   Amsinck reflected that his hop amounts may have been a little high for water which he initially believed to be hard. He seems to have had it analysed after he had brewed. Had he known, he says, he would have used less hops. His revised amounts are given in brackets.

He always argued that high carbonate hardness (caused by calcium hydrogen carbonate) required heavier hopping. This is at variance with his overnight liquor boil, which must have precipitated out his carbonate! I have always believed that high carbonate hardness produces additional harshness from hops. 10 brewers, 11 opinions? Something to discuss on the Internet. Let me know.

RECIPE 12 (HISTORICAL)

No. 30 in Amsinck's log

EAST INDIA PALE ALE
54/- PER BARREL

Another brew for which Amsinck decided to guess the water quality and another error of judgement by him. Amsinck finished the brew and then declared the water had been free of carbonate hardness after all. Very odd that he didn't realise earlier!

Amsinck writes, "This gyle, and all that followed for eight years, have proved most excellent. Since the gyle was brewed it was found that two thirds the quantity of hops would have been sufficient." (His revised figured are in brackets.)

This too was brewed in March.

ORIGINAL GRAVITY	1067		17° Plato	

WATER No analysis. Hard well.

	25 LITRES	23 LITRES	5 UK GALS	5 US GALS
New Pale	6.3 kg	5.8 kg	12.7 lb	10.3 lb

START OF BOIL
New choice East Kent. Goldings aroma 4.5% alpha-acid. Used in next day's brewing.

	340 g	313 g	15.7 oz	12.7 oz
	(226 g)	(207 g)	(10.3 oz)	(8.4 oz)

BREWING METHOD
Liquor boiled overnight and allowed to cool. Two infusion mashes and a sparge at 50°C (120°F). Sparge used as return wort. Use is not given. First to second mash ratio 1:1.8

First mash: Strike 74°C (165°F). Mashed and then stood 90 minutes. Settled at 65°C (149°F)

Second mash: Strike 82°C (180°F). Mashed and then stood 90 minutes. Settled at 74°C (165°F)

BOIL TIME 1st wort boiled 105 minutes, 2nd wort boiled 135 minutes and both worts then combined.

DRY HOP (CASK)

	94 g	86 g	3.1 oz	2.5 oz
	(61 g)	(57 g)	(2.0 oz)	(1.7 oz)

FERMENTATION   Pitched at 17°C (63°F). Rose to 23°C (73°F) during following 42 hours. Dropped to 1031 (8°P).

RACKING GRAVITY   Skimmed at intervals 3 hours, 4, 6, 9, and twice at 12 hourly intervals. After 5 days, transferred into kegs, dry hops added and closed.

ALCOHOL CONTENT   8.3% v/v   6.5% w/w

BITTERNESS   168 EBU (110 EBU). Probably not relevant.

COLOUR   3.5 EBC

COMMENTS   Amsinck boils and hops his return worts, even though they are to be used the next day for another beer. It seems that he reuses spent hops for a return wort and estimates what they would have been equivalent to, had they been fresh. Where he doesn't specify "new hops" he may have recycled old ones, but he wouldn't have done this in an IPA.

This explains why he was prepared to use such large quantities. He obviously recovered costs on a second, much inferior beer, or he used his thin run off liquor to mash a Porter the following day.

RECIPE 13 (HISTORICAL)

No. 31 in Amsinck's log

EAST INDIA PALE ALE. 60/- PER BARREL

Despite having an analysis for the mash liquor, Amsinck still ended up in a pickle, for the analysis was apparently incorrect or more likely, he doesn't seem to have read it properly or maybe he had it analysed after the event. Such errors can easily happen, as spring, pond and well water can change day for day, although that was less likely to be a problem in 1830 than nowadays, when we have the water network to contend with. Again he brewed in March. Another Scottish led gyle.

ORIGINAL GRAVITY 1064		16° Plato	

WATER   No. 11 analysis. Hard.

	25 LITRES	23 LITRES	5 UK GALS	5 US GALS
New Pale	5.7 kg	5.2 kg	11.8 lb	9.3 lb

START OF BOIL

New choice East Kent Goldings aroma 4.5% alpha-acid. Used in next day's brewing.

	296 g	272 g	10 oz	8 oz

BREWING METHOD

Liquor boiled overnight and allowed to cool. Two infusion mashes and a sparge at 82°C (180°F). Sparge combined with first wort. 2nd wort used as return wort. Boiled with same hops to make a table beer. First to second mash ratio 3:1.

First mash: Strike 73°C (163°F). Mashed and then stood 120minutes. Settled at 64°C (147°F). Sparged 10 litres (2 gallons)

Second mash: Strike 82°C (180°F). Mashed and then stood 60 minutes. Settled at 72°C (162°F)

BOIL TIME   1st wort boiled 90 minutes, 2nd wort boiled 120 minutes and both worts then combined.

DRY HOP (CASK)

	93 g	85 g	3.1 oz	2.5 oz

FERMENTATION   Pitched at 15°C (59°F). Rose to 22°C (71.5°F) during following 17 hours. Dropped to 1030 (7°Plato). Cleansed into butts.

RACKING GRAVITY   After 5 days dry hops added and closed in kegs.

ALCOHOL CONTENT   8.3% v/v   6.5% w/w

BITTERNESS   107 EBU. Probably not relevant.

COLOUR   4.0 EBC

COMMENTS   Amsinck thought this liquor more soft than it was and mashed 2°F lower than he would otherwise have done. "Notwithstanding, the Ale was as good as it was possible to be. This gyle strengthens my opinion that low heats make the finest flavoured Ale".

Due to Amsinck's error of judgement we learn another Victorian rule of thumb: mash hot in hard water but drop the temperature for soft. Contrast this with a modern rule of thumb, mash hot for flavour and cool for alcohol.

RECIPE 14 (HISTORICAL

No. 32 in Amsinck's log

NOVEMBER EAST INDIA PALE ALE
54/- PER BARREL

Another gloating ale. "As good as any from Burton."

On the water quality he wrote, "The Liquor, used in this Gyle, ran direct into the Liquor Back from the Hills."

Brewed in November.

ORIGINAL GRAVITY	1058		15° Plato	

WATER	No analysis. Hard hill water.			

	25 LITRES	23 LITRES	5 UK GALS	5 US GALS
New Derby Pale				
	5.8 kg	5.3 kg	11.6 lb	9.4 lb

START OF BOIL

New choice East Kent. Goldings aroma 4.5% alpha-acid. Used in next day's brewing.

	322 g	296 g	10.8 oz	8.8 oz

BREWING METHOD

Liquor boiled overnight and allowed to cool. Two infusion mashes. 2nd wort used as return wort. Boiled with same hops to make a table beer. First to second mash ratio 1:1.6

First mash: Strike 74°C (165°F). Mashed and then stood 120 minutes. Settled at 65°C (149°F).

Second mash: Strike 82°C (180°F). Mashed and then stood 60 minutes. Settled at 71°C (160°F)

BOIL TIME 1st wort boiled 90 minutes, 2nd wort boiled 90 minutes and both worts then combined.

DRY HOP (CASK)

	90 g	82 g	3.0 oz	2.4 oz

FERMENTATION Pitched at 20°C (68°F). Skimmed every few hours and attemperated. Rose to 21°C (70.5°F) during following 36 hours.

RACKING GRAVITY Dropped to 1029 (7°P). Racked into casks and dry hopped.

ALCOHOL CONTENT	8.2% v/v	6.4% w/w

BITTERNESS   116 EBU. Probably not relevant.

COLOUR   4.0 EBC

COMMENTS   Amsinck sparged a return wort at 160°F and used it in the next day's brewing. He reused the hops too, judging 90 lb spent hops to be the equivalent of 21 lb of those he had used the once.

This gyle is the weakest of any Amsinck IPAs.

RECIPE 15 (HISTORICAL)

No. 33 in Amsinck's log

INSTRUCTOR'S EAST INDIA PALE ALE 60/- PER BARREL

This gyle was brewed from only 2 quarters of malt, (approximately 500 lb). "Lilliputian" is Amsinck's adjective to describe it. Another March gyle brewed in Amsinck's own brewery by his "Pale Ale instructor." We have still to identify him.

ORIGINAL GRAVITY	1067	17° Plato

WATER	No analysis. Hard well water.

	25 LITRES	23 LITRES	5 UK GALS	5 US GALS
New Suffolk Pale				
	6.5 kg	6.0 kg	13.3 lb	10.7 lb

START OF BOIL

New choice East Kent Goldings aroma 4.5% alpha-acid. Used in next day's brewing.

	407 g	375 g	13.7 oz	11.1 oz

BREWING METHOD

Liquor boiled overnight and allowed to cool. Teaspoon of Plaster of Paris. Two infusion mashes. 2nd wort used as return wort. Boiled with same hops to make a table beer. First to second mash ratio 1:1.6

First mash: Strike 77°C (170°F). Mashed and then stood 120 minutes. Settled at 65°C (149°F).

Second mash: Strike 82°C (180°F). Mashed and then stood 60 minutes. Settled at 69°C (157°F)

BOIL TIME 1st wort boiled 105 minutes, 2nd wort boiled 165 minutes and both worts then combined.

DRY HOP (CASK)

	92 g	85 g	3.1 oz	2.5 oz

FERMENTATION Pitched at 18°C (68°F). Rose to 22°C (72°F) during following 12 hours.

RACKING GRAVITY Dropped to 1031 (8°P). Racked into kilderkins and dry hopped. Closed the same day.

ALCOHOL CONTENT	8.3% v/v	6.5% w/w

BITTERNESS   147 EBU. Probably not relevant.

COLOUR   4.0 EBC

COMMENTS   Despite its hardness, the instructor still added calcium sulphate, although he couldn't have known the water was deficient in this Burton salt. But gypsum is barely soluble in water and so one cannot overdose.

RECIPE 16 (HISTORICAL)

The Brewer 1866

BAVARIAN HOPS PALE BITTER ALE

This gyle is remarkable as it was brewed using one third Bavarian hops, which was not at all usual at the time for top quality ales, where, we are told, "For delicacy of flavour, foreign hops should be very sparingly employed." They seem to have been more common for the cheaper beers competing for the home market.

ORIGINAL GRAVITY 1062		15° Plato	

WATER   No analysis. Hard well water.

	25 LITRES	23 LITRES	5 UK GALS	5 US GALS
New Suffolk Pale				
	5.8 kg	5.4 kg	11.6 lb	9.4 lb

START OF BOIL

The hops were one third Bavarian (probably low alpha acid but high aroma), one third East Kent Goldings and one third Farnhams, probably again Goldings at around 4.5% alpha-acid.

407 g	375 g	13.7 oz	11.1 oz

BREWING METHOD

Two mashes were used but the second was only used as a return wort.

First mash: Strike 77°C (170°F). Mashed and then stood 120minutes. Settled at 65°C (149°F).

Second mash: Strike 82°C (180°F). Mashed and then stood 60 minutes. Settled at 69°C (157°F)

BOIL TIME   75 minutes. The hops were well broken and thoroughly mixed before use and were added at the beginning of the boil.

DRY HOP (CASK))

66 g	61 g	2.2 oz	1.8 oz

FERMENTATION   Pitched at 14°C (61°F). Rose to 19°C (66°F) over 4 days.

RACKING GRAVITY   Dropped to 1011 (3°P). Racked quite bright and dry hopped. Closed the same day.

ALCOHOL CONTENT		8.3% v/v	6.5% w/w

BITTERNESS   Impossible to estimate.

COLOUR   4.0 EBC

COMMENTS   We aren't told this beer was for export, but most worts for the domestic market were attenuated by this writer to 1014. This particular brew was left to drop to 1011 before racking, leading us to believe it wasn't for the domestic market. However, the hopping rate is only 18 lb per quarter, which was considered ample for a domestic beer but well below the export minimum of 21–23 lb per quarter. This is probably a classic IPA for the domestic market, and as such fell between stools.

RECIPE 17 (HISTORICAL)

(Researched and worked up by Durden Park Beer Circle.)

ORIGINAL INDIA PALE ALE 1837

This is described as a recipe which corresponds "to the heaviest IPA shipped from Burton in the 1830s". Simonds of Reading were shipping an almost identical formulation in 1880.

My thanks go to members of the Durden Park Beer Circle in West London for allowing me to use their work. I report the recipes as they are in their publication *Old British Beers and How to Make Them*.

ORIGINAL GRAVITY 1070 17° Plato

WATER Burton type.

	25 LITRES	23 LITRES	5 UK GALS	5 US GALS
Pale Malt	9.4 kg	8.7 kg	19.1 lb	15.5 lb
START OF BOIL Goldings 5% alpha-acid.				
	380 g	350 g	12.5 oz	10.1 oz
Dry hops	15 g	14 g	0.5 oz	0.4 oz

BREWING METHOD

- Add hot water to the ground grain to produce a stiff mash at 66°C (150°F)
- Maintain this temperature for 180 minutes.
- Raise the temperature to 77°C (170°F) for 30 minutes.
- Sparge slowly with water at 82–85 °C (182–185°F) to obtain the required volume.
- Boil with hops for 90 minutes.
- Cool, strain and rinse the hops.
- Adjust to the required gravity by adding cold boiled water or dried pale malt extract as needed.
- Ferment with a good quality Ale yeast.
- Dry hop with $\frac{1}{2}$ oz (15g) Goldings.
- Mature for at least 8 months.

ALCOHOL CONTENT	7.7% v/v	6.1%w/w

BITTERNESS	152 EBU

COLOUR	4.0 EBC

COMMENTS　　This is a heavily hopped ale, and the long maturation is essential to cure any hop astringency. John Harrison's notes on pale ale brewing water suggest a total salt content of 800–1000 ppm, mostly accounted for by calcium and sulphate ions but with small amounts of sodium and chloride ions present. Details on how to achieve this are included in the Appendix 2 notes on Murphy's water treatment.

Modern American and British IPAs

By the turn of the century, US brewers were muscling in on the IPA market. It was lucrative, and with the growth of their merchant fleet they were keen to fill the empty vessels returning to Asia. In fact many brewers had put up with the inconvenience of exporting ales, simply because the fleet owners made it worth their while. During the nineteenth century Great Britain was the world's manufacturing power-house. Huge amounts of raw material were being imported from the colonies, manufactured into goods to satisfy the domestic market and re-exported to Europe and the US. This left a huge unutilised tonnage returning to the colonies. Ship owners were keen to redress this problem and so exports such as beer were seen as a handy solution. Tom Tomlinson's research on US beer exports shows they were stronger than the UK equivalents of the time, ranging between 1065 and 1076 (16–19°P) at a time when UK export ales were stuck around the 1060–1065 mark (15–17°P).

There are no shortages of recipes for 20th century IPAs from both sides of the Atlantic. Unfortunately I have had to reject them all as being too dark, too lightly hopped or too low in Original Gravity to qualify as a genuine IPA. Many use dark malts, which is not right from the point of view of tradition. Furthermore pale beers are the hardest to brew. Dark malts can cover a multitude of sins. A strong pale ale leaves nowhere to hide. Other recipes use grits such as wheat malt, torrefied this and that, rice and white maize. James McCrorie told me the story of the interview he did with a retired Head Maltster from Edinburgh, who was a leading figure on the Scottish brewing scene. He was a very old man by then. When asked about the Scottish habit of using maize grits after around 1900 he received the answer, "James there were three reasons. Price, price and price."

Edinburgh brewers discovered that African maize was imported to Holland where the oil was extracted leaving useless, so the Dutch thought, grits. It was a short sea voyage from Rotterdam to Leith and well worth while to ship them across.

Later in the early 1950s an alternative source was found when the first UK production of corn flakes began. The process left huge quantities of undersized flakes, which were thought to be waste – until our Edinburgh head maltster heard about them! So apparently Scottish breweries in 1951 could pick up the grits for next to nothing and then stretch their mash very economically.

Now there is nothing wrong with grits, apart from the fact that they produce thin tasteless beer, although some brewers use them to dilute the high nitrogen content of inferior barley malt and in my own mind I'm sure they were excellent beers if you don't know better, but this book is about IPA, pale, strong and bitter, so I shall have to assign all those look alikes to subsequent publications on other types of ale and bitter.

Then again, several modern American micro-breweries, particularly in the North West states of Washington and Oregon, produce extremely highly hopped IPAs. However they have failed to appreciate the maturation requirement and their beers are truly medicinally bitter although they have a certain following as a counter to the lack of hop character in mainstream US beers.

Scottish Pale Ales and their Water

Scottish brewers around 1840 were adjured if possible to brew only with soft water. "Hard water will not have such free access to the malt," was Roberts' argument, "and fermentation proceeds much more equably with soft rather than hard water."

It is certainly true that all beers profit from being brewed with soft water, but some beers are simply more forgiving of hard liquor. Whilst many English writers spent their time assuring us that perfectly good ales can be brewed with hard water, there is little doubt as to the wisdom of soft water brewing. However, Victorian brewers would have been delighted with the purity and cleanliness of modern water and would have swapped their water gladly for a little chlorine that we have to put up with. There are no shortages of comments including "putrefaction," which would indicate the presence of dead plants and animals. Before the work of Pasteur, and for a long time after in remote areas, it was common to take brewing and dairy water from the same pond or stream at which cattle would drink and defecate. There are times when historical authenticity loses its charm!

Well water was least favoured by Roberts due to its hardness, which isn't to say that it wasn't used and many of us now have to deal with the modern equivalent of well water, i.e. water supplies which have their origins in ground water. And with the introduction of the national water grid, which allows water to be pumped from another part of the country to compensate for local shortages, we are quite likely to have different water supplies on consecutive days. A butt in the garden with a charcoal filter may yet be all that is left to serious brewers.

For those of us plagued with aggressive hard water, the natural solution is to reach for some darker malts, the chemistry of which helps mask the deficiencies in the water. As already stated, committed IPA brewers will not want to adopt this practice, and so may have to adhere more closely to the English recipes of the preceding chapter.

Ingredients North of the Border

All ingredients apart from water, posed a problem for Scottish brewers. The harsh climate does not allow for hops to be cultivated commercially and barley would not be planted out of choice. But if Whisky is your national drink, then domestic barley is a must. I venture to suggest, that Whisky distilling is more forgiving of poor barley than brewing is. I shall certainly have to put up with correction but there you are. The problem when dealing with matters Scottish, is that the people who really know what is what are not dispassionate, (anything but) mainly because they are Scottish. One doesn't really know whom to believe. I will be told that the best barley in the UK is grown in the 'Black Isle' region , north of Inverness – not really an island and that Alan Hay, of Taylor's Landlord fame, insisted on using 'Golden Promise' barley malt from Scotland. Nevertheless, in the year of writing, (2000) the Scots gave up on their grain harvest as a bad job. The dampness caused the grain to germinate whilst still in the ear, making it quite unusable. So let us generalise and try to keep out of hot mash water.

Scottish Brewers were faced with an import problem, maybe because so much domestic barley was demanded by the distilleries and maybe because the harvest was unreliable. Nowadays no one shows concern at bringing in goods by rail, lorry or sea, but 150 years ago this was no small undertaking and even more aggravating was that having purchased barley and transported it, what did you do with any batches which were deemed unsuitable? Make lower quality beers of course, which is why Scottish writers spend pages telling brewers how to test their barley and malt. This is itself not of particular interest to us, as reputable maltings will always provide reliable malt. The people to watch though are the retailers. You must be merciless with them and insist on seeing documentation on when the malt was delivered, especially if it is to be purchased ready crushed. Buy only unbroken sacks and never touch ready bagged small quantities.

A lot of barley was imported into Britain, and not just by

the Scots. The more forgiving climate around the Mediterranean for instance meant that lower nitrogen barley was more easily and reliably achieved. By the 1880s, areas around Norfolk receive the greatest praise among the domestic barleys, both in terms of climate and soil. Cold, clay and excessive precipitation, especially once the ear had formed, were considered to be the worst evils, which must cast doubt on the notion that Scotland produced significant amounts suitable for brewing. The most noted strain for brewers was Chevalier and that seems to have established itself in brewing legend by the turn of the century. That said, the quest for authentic ales may yet lead us to try to recapture these once used varieties and malt them ourselves. Many UK breweries throughout the nineteenth century purchased barley and malted it and the practice was certainly prevalent in Scotland. Brewing literature as late as 1904 provides us with designs for DIY domestic malters.

The information from Roberts on Scottish pale ale brewing, which is of special interest, is his note on the rate of extraction which pale ale brewers expected from first rate malt. "From a bushel of best malt, weighing forty pounds, twenty-six – nay even thirty pounds of fermentable matter may be extracted." This is useful for brewers who want to check their mash against historical literature. I'll tell you now though, those Scottish brewers of 150 years ago were no slouches when it came to mashing and sparging.

Hops attracted a lot of comment, especially before brewers had much idea how they worked and which chemicals did the business. Even modern brewers would admit that our present day understanding of the hop and its role in beer, is very incomplete. Surprisingly, the English predilection for Kent or going further back, for Farnham hops, does not receive universal acceptance. Nottingham "North-Clay hops", were described by Richardson as "rank, bordering on the nauseous." He wasn't in anyway perturbed by this matter, saying they were better suited to "strong keeping beers" than the more delicate Southerners. Hence the Scottish brewers may well have used hops of lower quality (by reputation and price only), because they were not prepared to pay the price differential and the additional transport involved in procuring Kent or Hampshire samples. We may be certain though that Edinburgh brewers *did* pay the extra and go for Home-Counties' varieties and there was good trade through the Clyde with North American hops. So we may assume that the Glasgow-Edinburgh corridor didn't do as Richardson suggested and use the nauseous north clay varieties. Once again, generalisations may be dangerous. One would have to investigate each brewery's records and then we may find there is no pattern that we can call "Scottish". The main concern was age, one year old hops being regarded as only fit for lesser quality beers. We should take a leaf from their book and challenge the retailer who still keeps his hops in plastic bags in the light. They remain so reluctant to put their house in order. Nothing but vacuum packed in thick aluminium foil will do unless you can be sure the retailer has a brisk turnover. If you get the opportunity to purchase good hops but the quantity is large, remember that they freeze well and IPAs use up lots.

Scottish Mashes

n Scottish literature the mash temperature raises its head again. "The great aim of brewers is that the wort, when it flows from the mash tun, shall range from 64–67°C (147–152°F)," wrote Roberts. "The wort parts freely from the goods, flowing transparently, and carrying a white pearly head." In order to be within this range by the time the tap is set, (the wort is run off) one needs a strike temperature considerably higher than this. Figures in the region of 82°C (180°F) abound and this would certainly be too warm in my brewery, but then breweries 150 years ago tended to be cold thick-walled places. I suggest 75°C is more appropriate.

Also of note is the fundamental difference used in Scottish breweries for beginning the strike. I have reported that the English tended to heat the liquor and then run it into the grist from underneath the false bottom. Not so in Scotland! The water was heated, run into the mash tun, allowed to cool to the right temperature and the grist then shot in with stirring, from a hopper. The only objection to this method was the waste of malt substance, as the farina, (fine dust) escapes from the mash tun. This is doubtless more of a nuisance than a waste, but nowadays we would also raise the objection of the brewer's labourer breathing in the fine dust. The older the malt, the more likely it is to contain mould spores and the more dangerous the practice. So although the Scots were quite adamant that their method was most efficacious, it is worth considering having some form of hood in place to prevent the dust escaping. This is what the English in fact did. Bottom mashing meant their grist did not need stirring as vigorously while being shot into the tun, and so a small trapdoor in the lid was a sufficient opening for the brewer to work through. This meant that the bulk of the dust remained within the mash tun.

Thus Roberts describes a Scottish IPA mash:
• "The average temperature of a brewery in Scotland in the brewing season is about 42°F (6°C) .
• The heat I take for the first mash, in those circumstances is 180°F (80°C), turning on for the first running, four fifths of the whole of the liquor I intend to use.
• After mashing (*stirring*) about twenty five minutes, I then turn

on the remaining one fifth on the goods, at an increase of 5°F (9°C) of heat, to make up for the loss of temperature which necessarily takes place during that time, and continue the mashing until it is finished (uniform temperature and wetness achieved). The time employed in mashing is generally forty to fifty minutes.
• When this process is completed about a bushel of grist is equally strewed on the surface of the mash, which, by forming a temporary paste, retains the heat and keeps up the temperature.
• The mash tun is then covered up and allowed to remain in that state for two to three hours, according to the heat of the air.
• The tap is then set and the wort run into the underback or into the wort copper."

In later editions, Roberts included a special chapter on India Beers and he devotes no less than three pages just to mashing heats. Much of what he says is not relevant to the small scale brewer, as our surface area to volume ratio is much less advantageous than for larger mashes. Hence we suffer from temperature drop to a larger extent than he did. I like the Victorian habit of strewing the liquor surface with another shovel of malt to help prevent heat loss through the exposed surface. It may also have served to prevent acetification. The malt was strewn as soon as the mash (stirring) was finished and the infusion (rest) was about to start.

What we can also rely on is Roberts' statement, "It has been satisfactorily ascertained, that if the heats of the worts, when about half run down into the under-back is from 145–150°F a judicious mashing heat has been employed for the first mash, and it is the brewer's object to attain this desired point." This would put the average IPA mash temperature at 63–66°C. This is very much at the bottom end of the temperature range for mashing, but does fit in with the old brewer's adage, "mash cool for strength and hot for flavour." I suppose there was no risk of IPAs under-achieving in the flavour department, and so the brewers concentrated on alcohol.

Scottish Sparging

As already stated, the Scottish brewer had, by the time of IPAs, dispensed with the multiple mashes still favoured in England and gone over to sparging. It is worth bearing in mind, that so-called second and third mashes were not mashes as we understand them. It is very unlikely that any further enzyme activity took place after the main mash and infusion, so subsequent mashes were really just wash processes. So the sparge was a natural step to take as it speeds up the wash process and is felt by many to be a more effective wash. Here again we find that a precise technique was involved, to which we should adhere if we are to recreate these magnificent ales.

• "The practice of the Scottish brewer is to commence sparging very soon after the tap is set, others commence to sparge immediately upon the tap being set and indeed some commence before they slack, and continue this operation without intermission until the desired quantity of extract has been obtained; the tap is allowed to run meanwhile, in order that the wort may run off in nearly the same proportion with the liquor which is sparged on.

• Others allow one fifth or more of the wort to run off before commencing with the sparge.

• The heat of the liquor employed for sparging is generally 10-20°C warmer than that used for the first mash," but for IPA's he writes in the 1847 edition, "I recommend the operation of sparging be commenced a minute or two after the taps are opened, and for this particular beer (IPA) sparge with liquor ranging from 185–190°F (85–88°C).

• The surface of the goods must not become exposed or acetification can occur."

Victorian mash arms were far superior to anything that modern home brewers can buy. All commercially available small scale sparge arms available to the modern home brewer cannot allow for the fact that as the water head from the copper reduces, so does the turning moment of the arm. Hence Scottish brewers had spargers with a shallow cup sitting on them, into which the liquor was run. Provided the depth in the cup was kept around constant, the water discharged onto the goods remained about the same. This is important, as too little water may have allowed the surface to become dry, the grain to go off in the warm damp atmosphere, and then vinegary flavours subsequently be washed into the wort. Too much water causes flooding of the goods and one may as well second mash. A more modern solution to the problems of flow rate is to use a low through-put pump.

We of course work on a much smaller scale than Victorian brewers and so the time scales for sparging with much less water are much smaller and naturally the dangers of bacterial oxidation to vinegar is correspondingly reduced. Nevertheless, I have observed in our modern humdrum life, we are only too keen to take time off for other jobs and leave a sparge to its own devices. This is not a good idea for making a noble beer and if this course of action is necessary, I advise multiple mashes.

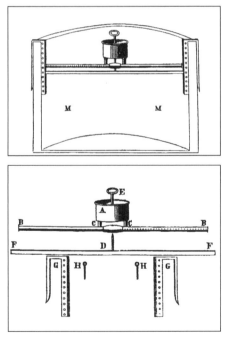

Sparging Scottish style in the 19th century.

131

Scottish Worts

Boiling of worts in Scotland seems never to have exceeded 1½ hours, which was generally shorter than for English recipes. This doubtless kept the ales paler. A common bittering hop addition was 6 lb for a quarter of malt, which is much closer to the English average, with the notable exception of Amsinck who, we should remember, added huge quantities, in the manner of early IPA brewing. Roberts also owns that Scottish brewers used to use closer to 10 lb/quarter when brewing from January to March and with worts around 1095 to 1100.

"Four pounds of the hops were put into the copper when the wort was around 200°F (93°C) of heat and boiled very briskly for the space of around 20 minutes; the remaining six pounds were then added, and allowed to boil for thirty or forty minutes, according to the circumstances.

It will be observed, that the quantity of hops we made use of exceeds the proportion generally allowed by Scottish brewers, and that, in the example given, no portion of the hops was put into the copper until the wort was within a few degrees of the boiling point; and until this portion had boiled for 20 minutes, the remainder was not added. The result was that we obtained for the finer ales the more delicate flavour of the hops."

Roberts goes on to supply the following rates for pale strong ales (1838):

SG	Plato	R	TC	L1	L2	
1095	24	4:6	10	20	40	
1085	21	4:4	8	15	40	
1075	19	2:5	7	20	40	

But when writing in 1847 specifically about India Ales he recommends:

SG	Plato	R	TC	L1	L2	
1068	17	3:4	14(22)	20	50	

R=Ratio of hops per boil period (lb);
TC=Total copper hops per quarter (lb)
L1=Length of boil period one; L2=Length of boil period two

So the Scottish hopping rates seem considerably lower than those used in England. He acknowledges Burton brewers used 20–22 lb per quarter whereas the Scots use 16–18 lb per quarter. However, upon checking his arithmetic I find he used 22 lb per quarter too, for he always had to do two boilings as his copper was not large enough to boil everything at once, and he kept back another 8 lb per quarter for the second wort.

To summarise then:
- He added hops to the wort when within a few degrees of boiling.
- He added 27% of his copper hop total immediately.
- He added just over 37% after 20 minutes and boiled for a further 50 minutes.
- Another 36% was kept back for the second wort.

Therefore, as we shall probably boil only the once, if we work on one quarter of the hop total added immediately and three quarters after twenty minutes, and then boil for fifty minutes, we shall emulate his method.

Another point of interest is that although the Scots seemed to have had the latest sparge technology under their belts, they hadn't bothered with a hop back, but persevered with filtering through hair cloth filters to remove the hop waste. This removed only the largest hop particles and allowed much of the smaller hop impurities to be carried along with the wort into the fermenter. There can be little doubt that this affected the final product and Scottish brewers of the time were not sure in their own minds whether this was a good or bad thing. Presumably the English were convinced of the advantage of a clear bright uncontaminated wort in the fermenter, but maybe this was just because they had spent the money on hop backs and were not about to declare them superfluous.

Some Scots were however employing spiral cooler pipes running through cold water. This caused much of the retained soluble and insoluble material to precipitate or settle out. Maybe they arrived at the same point as the English. Many more breweries both sides of the Border persevered with cooling in large open flat trays, sometimes of iron, sometimes of wood. This must have caused oxidation of the wort and considerable risk of infection. Either material would not have been inert and would have imparted its own flavour. Open coolers, iron or wood, are not options I'd like to try.

Cool Fermentations

There was also some considerable variation in fermenting temperatures either side of the Border. The English were renowned for starting their fermentations at relatively high temperatures. This makes some sense as parts of England can be very humid and mild, even in the early or late part of the year and in England we do feel the urge to get our fermentations off to a flyer. In most of Scotland the midsummer temperatures would be considered cool for a top fermentation and attemperation is never a problem. So according to Roberts, the English had been known to start fermentations at between 24–27°C (75–80°F) (albeit the top end of the ranges was a rarity) but the Scots would not err outside the range 4–14 °C (44–58°F) and then the lower temperature was the rarity. Of course the Scots would tie up a fermenter for anything up to three weeks for such a cool gyle, whilst the English would hardly exceed six days. By the 1840s Scottish Ales were in such demand in England and indeed world wide, that the Scots had to curtail their long cool fermentations in order to maximise their turnover and investment. So by 1847 the Scots were fermenting India Ales warmer and closer to English temperatures.

- The worts were rarely in the tun longer than 24–30 hours.
- They were then roused and cleansed into hogsheads and attenuated down to 1024.
- To achieve this they were pitched at 58–60 °F (14–16°C) and the fermenting gyle gained around 7°F (3°C) during fermentation.
- Cask fermentation was completed within 14–20 days.

The Scots apparently never skimmed their head from the fermenting liquor. Our English recipes from Amsinck indicate that he frequently skimmed. The removal of the hop resins and the foam itself does seem to diminish the effects of the bittering so the extreme hop quantities suggested by Amsinck may have had something to do with his predilection for skimming. The Scots in fact would wait for the foam head to reach its most rocky magnificence, and then beat it in, in this way presumably increasing the effect of the hop bittering agents.

Scottish Historical Recipes

Domestic brewing; a Hand Book for Families of 1839, gave the following definition of a Scottish Ale. I have paraphrased.

• Very pale, very mild, hop head never prevailing.

• Very strong. Close to a French Pale wine, caused by fermenting it in the same manner as those wines, i.e. with a very cool lengthened fermentation. Can only be done in cold times of year,

• Very pale malt of only the highest quality.

• Hops were Farnham or East Kent

• The Scotch practice is to make only one mash, very stiff, with liquor heated to at least 180°F if not 190°F, varying with dampness of malt.

• Mash for 20–30 minutes, cover and rest for three hours.

• Make up the quantity of wort with sprinklings called sparges. These sparges trickle progressively through the goods and wash out much more of the saccharine matter. This assumes a good mash has completely converted all sugar to starch.

• Run off the first wort and sparge with water at 180°F.

• These brews are sometimes adulterated with a little honey and coriander seeds.

• They are fermented at 45-50°F which eliminates vinous fermentation.

• They are allowed to warm by up about 12-15°F (to the ambient temperature) in the fermentation house.

• These ales become fine and are seldom racked for home market.

The above description gives us a starting point when looking for the definitive Scottish IPA and then the name "Roberts" occurs everywhere.

Roberts' IPAs are probably the definitive genre recipes of the nineteenth century. The reason for saying they were definitive, rests on the fact that the Scots were the first to try to rationalise the whole brewing process, e.g. they introduced sparging as an attempt to get round the inconvenience of brewing being essentially a batch process. They also realised the importance of pale malt. Until coal firing allowed controlled heating of the green malt, the colour of malt had always been a bit hit and miss. Heating material had always been at a premium and so old maltsters burned what was to hand. Exceptionally dry faggot wood had the tendency to burn or crystallise the outside of the grain. This inevitably led to a darkening of the beer, but because the optical opinion is always that dark beers are stronger than pale, brewers were quite happy to tolerate the darker varieties. As already mentioned, the advent of the hydrometer meant that brewers could measure their extract and the Scottish brewers quickly realised that dark malts were much a waste of time and money, so they started perfecting the pale ale for economic reasons.

The story goes that the greatest nineteenth century microbiologist Pasteur, took the trouble to visit the Younger's Brewery in Edinburgh and looked at their laboratory set up, with which they monitored their brewing success. Pasteur apparently gave them five stars for their competence.

The India Pale Ales from Scotland were monsters of beers, of incredible gravity and bitterness. Every home brewer should have tried one in his lifetime before he hangs up his mashing oar for the last time.

Roberts quotes two examples in his 1838 treatise. I've decided to give the first in its entirety and then the scaled down versions of both, for the home brewer.

Please note that "L5" stands for £5 or a "100/- ale".

EXAMPLE NO. 1

March 1, 1836 – L5 Ale. – Malt, 20 Quarters; – Hops, 160 lbs – Temperature 42°.

Commenced brewing at 4 A.M. by turning into the mash tun thirty two barrels of liquor at 200°. When reduced in temperature to 182°, shot twenty quarters of pale malt into the mash tun; and raked and mashed with oars forty-five minutes. Finished mashing at 5ho 15 min., and strewed a bushel of grist over mash and covered up. At 8 o'clock set tap, (or as they term it in Scotland, *slacked*,) uncovered and commenced sparging at the same time, with liquor at 190°, and continued the operation until thirty-two barrels were sparged. Wort running quite fine with good appearance; temperature 148° and 110 gravity. At 11ho 30 min., ale wort all in copper which gauged 48 barrels, at gravity 83, Allan's Saccharometer. Previously, however, shut tap and sparged on mash fifteen barrels of liquor for table beer.

Weighed one hundred and sixty lbs of the best East Kent hops, and put them to the wort in the copper ; at 12 wort came through , boiled briskly one hour and twenty-five minutes, and at 1ho 30 min. cast copper. At 2ho 30 min spread in coolers. At 10 o'clock P.M. pitched tun with eight gallons and a half of store weighing 90 lb, and let down wort at 50°, which gauged in the tun thirty-six barrels and a half, gravity 103.5.

The following table shows the heat of the tun during fermentation:–

March	o'clock	A.M./P.M.	Temperature °F
2	1	P.M.	50
3	9	A.M.	50
4	9	A.M.	52
5	8	A.M.	56
6	10	A.M.	58
7	8	A.M.	58.5
8	8	A.M.	59
9	8	A.M.	60
10	8	A.M.	61
11	8	A.M.	62.5
12	8	A.M.	63
13	8	A.M.	63
14	8	A.M.	63
15	8	A.M.	62

March 15.– Removed gyle from the tun into the square, the
  temperature of which when let down was 62°, and   gravity
  43.

March 16, 10 A.M.– Cleansed into hogsheads and barrels.

The summary of the forgoing example is as follows:–

Ale

36 barrels, at gravity 103.5 = 3726

Beer

10 barrels at gravity 40 = 400

3726 + 400 = 4126

Quarters of malt used   20

Value extracted from each quarter   206.3

This is in contrast to English recipes, and many Scottish brewing records, which provide only a minimum of detail. Everyone of the time was completely hung up on tables of fermentation heats. Brewers were still struggling to keep heats down, for the fermentation is exothermic and we small scale brewers forget the difficulty of dissipating heat from a large but low surface area volume of liquid. In fact this fermentation ran at 20°F above ambient. It was only by describing every step, including the weather and the quality of the bowel movement of the brewer, that early scientists were able to get an understanding of what was important and what to ignore. The nineteenth-century brewers were the world's first genuine micro-biologists. Here is a version for the modern kitchen of Roberts' mighty brew.

Scottish Recipe Section

Recipes 18 to 25 follow in this section.

RECIPE 18 (HISTORICAL)

Roberts' L5 ale 1839

ROBERTS' 100/- SCOTTISH PALE ALE

Roberts' first example of a Scottish pale ale was not designated for export. Judging by the strength and bittering it was certainly a forerunner of what was to come. It is the only commercial pale ale recipe I've found with a starting gravity in excess of 1100 (excepting his £7 Ale).

The method doesn't see the use of dry hopping as necessary, but the copper hopping quantities are considerable.

ORIGINAL GRAVITY	1103		26° Plato	
	25 LITRES	**23 LITRES**	**5 UK GALS**	**5 US GALS**
Pale Malt	11.8 kg	10.9 kg	23.9 lb	19.4 lb

START OF BOIL

Goldings 5% alpha-acid.

	294 g	270 g	10 oz	8 oz

DRY HOP (CASK)	Not applied

BREWING METHOD

- Bring the mash liquor to the boil.
- When the liquor in the mash tun cools to 83°C (182°F) shoot in the malt and bring the temperature to 65°C (148°F).
- Mash for 45 minutes.
- Strew malt over the surface (to insulate) and rest for 165 minutes.
- Begin running off the wort and sparging at the same time, so as to keep the surface wet.
- Cease running off at gravity 1083 (21°P).
- Transfer to the copper and add the hops.
- Bring to the boil and boil for 85 minutes.
- Cool the wort. The gravity should be around 1103.
- Pitch with a good working yeast and ferment out. This may take up to 14 days at 16°C (61°F).
- Cleanse into kegs and lay down for at least 1 year.

RACKING GRAVITY	1043	11°P

ALCOHOL CONTENT   10% v/v   7.5% w/w

BITTERNESS   The long maturation means the bittering will soften to produce other flavours.

COLOUR   4 EBC

COMMENTS   When I attempted to make this monster brew, I used Pipkin pale malt from Fawcett's of Castleford. It was rated at 5.5 EBU, in other words, far too dark for an IPA, but was otherwise excellent malt! My first run was well over 1100, the exact measure couldn't be taken as my hydrometer bulb was out the wort. The second run was at 1056 and they were combined for boiling, along with 400g of my own grown hops. This mixing of worts was an error of judgement, as I ended up with a starting gravity around 1082, which was considerable but less than Robert's 1103!

At home-brew hop prices, historical IPA brewers had better get used to growing their own! The Fawcett's malt was such good value and had I had to pay for the hops, they would certainly have exceeded the cost of the malt. Details on home hop cultivation are in The Craft of House-Brewing by Clive La Pensée

At the finish of the boil I had about 35 litres at 1090. I filled one Cornelius, aerated and pitched a good working Lalamand Pale London Ale Yeast. The fermentation started at around 16°C (61°F) but was allowed to rise to 20°C (68°F) over the following week. An air lock was used.

What to do with the remaining liquor in the copper exercised me. I discharged it into a second Cornelius Keg, diluted it down to 1055 with cold air-saturated water, and pitched a working Saflager Yeast. At the time of writing the jury is still waiting to sample the fruits of my labours.

RECIPE 19 (HISTORICAL)

Roberts' £7 Pale Ale

ROBERTS' 140/– SCOTTISH PALE ALE

Roberts second example of a Scottish pale ale was also not designated for export. He used so much malt that he was easily able to get a 30/– Ale out the sparge liquor.

ORIGINAL GRAVITY 1129			32° Plato

	25 LITRES	23 LITRES	5 UK GALS	5 US GALS
Pale Malt	16 kg	14.7 kg	32.3 lb	26.2 lb

START OF BOIL

Goldings 5% alpha-acid.

	403 g	371 g	13.5 oz	11 oz

DRY HOP (CASK)   Not applied

BREWING METHOD

- When the liquor in the mash tun cools to 84°C (183°F) shoot in the malt and bring the temperature to 65°C (149°F).
- Mash for 20 minutes.
- Turn on another 2½ litres (1 gallon) of water at 85°C (185°F).
- Mash for 15 minutes
- Strew malt over the surface (to insulate) and rest for 200 minutes.
- Begin running off the wort and sparging at 85°C (185°F) at the same time, so as to keep the surface wet.
- Cease running off at gravity 1105 (26°P).
- Transfer to the copper and add the hops.
- Bring to the boil and boil briskly for 85 minutes.
- Cool the wort. The gravity should be around 1129.
- Pitch with a good working yeast and ferment out. This may take up to 14 days at 16°C (61°F).
- Cleanse into kegs and lay down for at least 1 year.

RACKING METHOD   Not recorded

ALCOHOL CONTENT   11.3% v/v   8.9% w/w

BITTERNESS   The long maturation means the bittering will soften to produce other flavours.

COLOUR   4 EBC

COMMENTS Roberts' 60/- Ale, which he fermented with the sparge liquor, was a mere 1072 OG (18°P), which one may think, went extremely cheap at £3 per barrel. My second runnings from such monster brews (remember, I'm a second masher, not a sparger) have nothing like the sweetness which one would expect from their gravity. I assume that sparging or second mashing, extracts mainly the less soluble higher sugars. More research please!

RECIPE 20 (HISTORICAL)

(Researched and worked up by Durden Park Beer Circle)

USHER'S INDIA PALE ALE 1885

This is described as "a clean, bitter, refreshing pale ale". My thanks go to members of the Durden Park Beer Circle in West London for allowing me to use their work. I report the recipes as they are in their publication "Old British Beers and How to Make Them."

ORIGINAL GRAVITY 1060		15° Plato	

WATER	Burton type.		

	25 LITRES	23 LITRES	5 UK GALS	5 US GALS
Lager Malt	6.4 kg	5.9 kg	13 lb	10.5 lb

START OF BOIL
Goldings 5% alpha-acid.

	230 g	210 g	7.5 oz	6.1 oz

DRY HOPS

	15 g	14 g	0.5 oz	0.4 oz

BREWING METHOD

- Add hot water to the ground grain to produce a stiff mash at 66°C (150°F)
- Maintain this temperature for 180 minutes.
- Raise the temperature to 77°C (170°F) for 30 minutes.
- Sparge slowly with water at 82–85°C (182–185°F) to obtain the required volume.
- Boil with hops for 90 minutes.
- Cool, strain and rinse the hops.
- Adjust to the required gravity by adding cold boiled water or dried pale malt extract as needed.
- Ferment with a good quality ale yeast.
- Dry hop with $\frac{1}{2}$ oz (15g) Goldings.
- Mature for 8–9 months.

ALCOHOL CONTENT	6% v/v	4.8% w/w

BITTERNESS 92 EBU

COLOUR 4.0 EBC

COMMENTS This is a much later Victorian India Ale and we notice the radical reduction in hop quantities compared to some of the early Victorian gyles. This may be down to parsimony on the part of the brewer (which Amsinck regularly complained of) or technology meant that the beers kept better. It must also be worth asking by how much the voyage times had reduced between 1830 and 1890, meaning the beers didn't have to keep so long or whether the use of iron in ship building meant that the holds were closer to the water temperature than the air temperature in the tropics. There seems to be plenty of room for some social history research here. Comments are always welcome!

The use of lager malt is in deference to the difficulties in obtaining white malt or genuine pale malt.

RECIPE 21 (HISTORICAL)

(Researched and worked up by Durden Park Beer Circle)

YOUNGER'S EXPORT ALE OF 1848

This is described as "a medium gravity India type pale ale". My thanks go to members of the Durden Park Beer Circle in West London for allowing me to use their work. I report the recipes as they are in their publication "Old British Beers and How to Make Them."

ORIGINAL GRAVITY 1060	15° Plato

WATER   Burton type.

	25 LITRES	23 LITRES	5 UK GALS	5 US GALS
Pale Malt	6.2 kg	5.7 kg	12.5 lb	10.1 lb

START OF BOIL

Goldings 5% alpha-acid.

	356 g	330 g	11.7 oz	9.4 oz

DRY HOPS

	15 g	14 g	0.5 oz	0.4 oz

BREWING METHOD

- Add hot water to the ground grain to produce a stiff mash at 66°C (150°F)
- Maintain this temperature for 180 minutes.
- Raise the temperature to 77°C (170°F) for 30 minutes.
- Sparge slowly with water at 82–85°C (182–185°F) to obtain the required volume.
- Boil with hops for 90 minutes.
- Cool, strain and rinse the hops.
- Adjust to the required gravity by adding cold boiled water or dried pale malt extract as needed.
- Ferment with a good quality ale yeast.
- Dry hop with $\frac{1}{2}$ oz (15g) Goldings.
- Mature for at least 8 months.

ALCOHOL CONTENT	6% v/v	5% w/w

BITTERNESS	142 EBU

COLOUR	4.0 EBC

COMMENTS This recipe was taken from a Younger's brewing journal and is very low on detail. The brewer of the time knew what he was doing and couldn't imagine that anyone else wouldn't know (or would want to know)! Appendix 6 shows an extract from a typical brewing journal of the time from Younger's Brewery. This was kindly loaned me by the University of Glasgow Archives and gives some idea how difficult and painstaking the work of people like John Harrison and James McCrorie has been.

This is of course a Scottish recipe, and should be brewed with the notes on Scottish Ales, which precede these recipes. Hence there is reason to believe that it was a gyle which had relied on sparging for extract, rather than the English multiple mashing system. In fact Durden Park members have carried out some research into the two methods and found the product of either process to be virtually the same, all other parameters taken into account. This is good news, as it leaves us the latitude to choose whichever method is most convenient. I shall remain a double masher. I then use the second, much weaker return wort to regulate the gravity of my first wort.

RECIPE 22 (HISTORICAL)

(Researched and worked up by Durden Park Beer Circle)

YOUNGER'S IMPERIAL ALE 1835

"A high quality pale ale," is the terse description that this beer earns. The word "Imperial" suggests a colonial connection. Its parameters indicate that it may have been brewed for the domestic market, but obviously with the strength and bittering associated with an India Ale. My thanks go to members of the Durden Park Beer Circle in West London for allowing me to use their work.

ORIGINAL GRAVITY	1080	20° Plato

WATER No analysis.

	25 LITRES	23 LITRES	5 UK GALS	5 US GALS
Pale Malt	7.4 kg	6.8 kg	15 lb	12.2 lb

START OF BOIL

Goldings 5% alpha-acid.

	253 g	232 g	8.3 oz	6.7 oz

DRY HOPS

	15 g	14 g	0.5 oz	0.4 oz

BREWING METHOD

- Add hot water to the ground grain to produce a stiff mash at 66°C (150°F)
- Maintain this temperature for 180 minutes.
- Raise the temperature to 77°C (170°F) for 30 minutes.
- Sparge slowly with water at 82–85°C (182–185°F) to obtain the required volume.
- Boil with hops for 90 minutes.
- Cool, strain and rinse the hops.
- Adjust to the required gravity by adding cold boiled water or dried pale malt extract as needed.
- Ferment with a good quality ale yeast.
- Dry hop with $\frac{1}{2}$ oz (15g) Goldings.
- Mature for at least 8 months.

ALCOHOL CONTENT	8.8% v/v	6.9% w/w

BITTERNESS　　　100 EBU

COLOUR　　　4.0 EBC

COMMENTS　　　This is a much less heavily hopped ale, and relied on the high alcohol content to allow it to keep.

Durden Park research suggests that by the time of this IPA brewing, the vast variety of traditional English hops had dwindled to Fuggles and Goldings. Farnham Pale, easily the most prized early IPA hop was probably just another Fuggles by the 1880s. John Harrison assumes that we may as well just utilise Fuggles at around 4.5% alpha-acid bittering and Goldings at around 5.5%. I have assumed an average of 5% when calculating EBUs. Over the years, many varieties have made an appearance on the market, but few if any of these are resurrections of traditional strains.

RECIPE 23 (HISTORICAL)

"Recorded in Balham May 2000"

BALHAM IPA

There weren't many sunny Saturdays in May 2000, but I remember this one with particular delight. James McCrorie had agreed to read this manuscript and I invited myself down to discuss his thoughts. Before I arrived, he scoured his cellar for IPAs from the world over. We sat and worked in his garden and he poured one after the other, and of course served several of his own special oeuvres. This ale only finds its way out of the English section for one reason, the name. Not Balham, McCrorie. In fact I'm sure that its pedigree is North of the Border and is a spin off from James' research into Scottish Ale brewing and particularly Majority Ales. It was without doubt the best of his world selection he had on offer and the original length was 12 gallons. I give the scaled down parameters, directly from James' brewing log.

Original Gravity	1055		14° Plato	

WATER Use Murphy's Liquor treatment .

	25 LITRES	23 LITRES	5 UK GALS	5 US GALS
Maris Otter Pale				
	5.25 kg	4.8 kg	10.5 lb	8.5 lb

LIQUOR VOLUME

	18.75 litres	17.25 litres	3.75 gal	3.75 gal

COPPER HOPS

Goldings Early Bird. Alpha-acid 5.5%

START OF BOIL

	100 g	93 g	3.5 oz	2.7 oz

After 60 minutes

	50 g	46 g	1.7 oz	1.3 oz

After 75 minutes

	$1/_2$ teaspoon Irish Moss			

After 90 minutes

	45 g	42 g	1.5 oz	1.3 oz

DRY HOP (CASK)

	30 g	28 g	1.0 oz	0.8 oz

BREWING METHOD (parameters for 12 gallons)

- Strike temperature: 72°C (162°F)
- Malt (25 lb) at temperature 19°C (66°F)
- Liquor Volume: 9 gallons
- Mashed at 68°C (155°F) for 90 minutes.
- Wort cleared by 10 minutes very gentle recirculation.
- Tap set and first runnings taken at 1080.
- 10 gallons run off in 40 minutes. Gravity 1038.
- Sparge started after 15 minutes.
- Stopped running at 14 gallons at 1024. Total volume gravity was 1060.

BOIL TIME

- Boiled for 60 minutes with 8 oz Goldings Early Bird.
- Added further 4 oz Goldings and boiled for 15 minutes.
- Added further 1 heaped teaspoon Irish Moss.
- Boiled for further 15 minutes.
- After the boil there was 12 gallons at 1072.
- Made up to 14 gallons with hot liquor.
- Added 4 oz Goldings and brought back to low boil and switched off.
- Stood 30 minutes to let hops infuse.
- Inserted coil immersion cooler and brought to 22°C (72°F)
- Stood 60 minutes to settle hops and trub to a filter bed.
- Produced 11 gallons at 1060. Added cool liquor to make 12 gallons at 1055.

FERMENTATION

- Ran wort off the hops and trub.
- Oxygenated with 5 x 1 minute bursts of oxygen at 2 litres per minute through a sterile filter.
- Pitched with started yeast at 22°C (72°F) and controlled at this temperature.
- First activity observed after 6 hours. Full yeast head after 12 hours. Rocky after 14 hours.
- 1016 after 7 days and dropped into Cornelius Kegs.
- Secondary fermentation completed after a further 3 days. Dropped to 1012.
- Racked into Cornelius Kegs containing 1 oz Goldings for dry hopping and rolled twice daily for the following 7 days.
- Drank as soon as clear.

151

RACKING GRAVITY	1012	3ºP
ALCOHOL CONTENT	6% v/v	4$\frac{1}{2}$% w/w
BITTERNESS	88 EBU	
COLOUR	4.0 EBC	

COMMENTS   Before James founded the Craft Brewing Association he had the time to be a keen off-shore yachtsman. The story goes that he stowed a Cornelius of his IPA on his yacht and sailed it around the Solent and across the English Channel a few times over a period of 3 months or so, in order to see what the rocking motion would do for the beer. (Unfortunately the Solent is nowhere near warm enough for this exercise to imitate a trip through the tropics, and this was really a light-hearted experiment) but he thinks three summer months in the boot of his car, travelling round London, may get as close as is possible. He does not really think it will improve the beer. I await his results!

The dry hops were in a loosely woven muslin bag with two large stainless steel nuts. The keg was rolled daily and this caused considerable agitation and distribution of the flavourings.

You may be wondering about the OG for this Ale. A bit on the low side after all we've said. Maybe it is closer to a pale ale and he prefers it to be called "Golden Early Bird" after the colour and the hops.

RECIPE 24

It goes without saying, that the excellent IPAs of that May Saturday were accompanied by something good to eat. The *Oxford Dictionary* says the following of Kedgeree. "An Indian dish of rice boiled with split pulse, onions, eggs, and condiments, also in European cookery a dish made of cold fish, boiled rice, eggs and condiments, served hot. From the Hindi khichri, 1625." I thoroughly recommend it for any IPA party of like minded craft brewers, to complement your beer.

JAMES' KEDGEREE

- This recipe should be enough for four reasonable servings.
- $1\frac{1}{2}$ lb. (700g) thick smoked haddock. It really must be the proper, lightly coloured stuff not the ghastly brightly coloured dyed and smoke-flavoured version often seen.
- Place the fish, trimming it to size if necessary, into a broad saucepan or deep frying pan and cover it with 1 pint of water (or half water and half milk). Bring gently to the boil and then simmer gently for 4 minutes. Leave it to rest for another 5 minutes before draining off, and saving the cooking liquor.
- Leave the haddock to cool whilst you get on with the next bit.
- Boil 6 oz (170g) dry Basmati rice, together with a tablespoon of fennel seeds if you have them, in the cooking liquor for 4 minutes by which time the rice should be slightly undercooked. If using another type of rice the time will be longer or shorter. Then drain the rice and seeds. I sometimes save a little of the fish liquor and make up the boiling liquid with more water.
- Now sweat a large, not too finely, chopped onion and 3 crushed cloves of garlic in a generous amount of unsalted butter adding, after a few minutes, a heaped tablespoon of fish masala or a garam masala mix which has not too much chilli as part of the ingredients. Whilst I like a hot curry as much as anyone, the aim is to have the kedgeree spicy but not to overwhelm the haddock. Cook the mixture for about a further minute.
- By now the fish should be cool enough to handle so skin and de-bone it as you flake the fish.
- Combine the flaked fish, the drained rice with the onion, garlic and spice mix and gently fold together in a ceramic or metal pot. If the mixture seems a little dry, add any saved fish liquor. Place more than a few pats of unsalted butter on top and cover with a lid or foil. Place in a cool oven, about 120°C, and cook gently for 20 minutes or so. This allows the flavours to 'marry'. Gently mix the mixture before serving. If it seems dry-add more butter!
- Traditionally, kedgeree is served with a sprinkling of chopped hard boiled eggs and chopped parsley or coriander but usually I don't bother.

- I like mine with the balance of haddock to rice in favour of the fish but with lots of onions and especially a generous amount of butter. I usually make a large batch and freeze it as it can be easily microwaved when the urge arises or when you have visitors such as Clive, when the talking and drinking leave little time for cooking. Once you have made one batch you can easily adjust the recipe to your own taste.

For a posher version, see Susan Nowak's excellent book *The Beer Cook Book*, published by Faber & Faber and available from CAMRA Books (01727 867201).

Thanks James!

The famous nineteenth-century writer Mrs. Beeton, in her *Household Management* supplies another four varieties of this recipe for fish, paprika, meat and salmon. I think we have the makings of a cult IPA/Kedgeree movement.

My IPAs, brewed within the spirit of this book, taste sensational and it is a very good job that they are keeping beers, for I believe a six gallon keg will last a very long time, judging by the size glasses, which seem appropriate.

And here is a very last thought on Victorian drinking culture and an example of all the things we have yet to discover and try. In order to get some idea of drinking habits at the peak of IPA drinking in the UK, I turned to Charles Dicken's *The Old Curiosity Shop*. There I found Mr Richard Swiveller, raconteur, bon vivant and ne'r-do-well. Dick is the most human of characters in the novel, constantly finding new ways of getting his much loved Ale on tick, he never having any money of his own. In the cellar scene with the Marchioness, actually an ill-used orphan waif, he introduces us to a beverage called Purl. This was quite unknown to me but the *Oxford Dictionary* came to my aid. "A liquor made by infusing wormwood or other bitter herbs in ale or beer; later a mixture of hot beer with gin (also called *dog's nose*), sometimes also with ginger and sugar; in repute as a morning draught."

So, any feedback on this book should be e-mailed to:

dickswiveller@beeb.net

No post please, if you want an answer.

And here to end is the strongest beer recipe I have ever come across. It wasn't brewed for export but would have been laid down for a special occasion, such as the birth of a child, or maybe brewed in a year when the barley harvest was outstanding, and as such, became a way of preserving produce from bounteous years. So after IPA and Purl, let Cookbook Strong Ale put an end to this excess of Victorian excesses.

COOKBOOK STRONG ALE

This ale is early Victorian, from Every Family's Cookery Book. It is undated and the authoress is simply described "By an Experienced Cook." Perhaps she feared litigation. It is the strongest beer I've ever come across and from its gravity and hop rate, must have been an awesome ale, capable of withstanding the rigours of export. I have doubts if it was ever brewed. It uses half as much malt again per gallon as Roberts' 140/- Pale Ale.

The authoress indicated that for normal ales only two thirds the malt quantity should be taken, and that would put this ale on a par with the Scottish 140/- Ale. Of course there has to be a minimum amount of water one can take in order to wet the goods. This recipe must surely be getting close to that point and this may have been just another way of making three ales from one mash.

Another March gyle.

ORIGINAL GRAVITY Not known

WATER   No Analysis

	25 LITRES	23 LITRES	5 UK GALS	5 US GALS
Pale Malt	24.8 kg	22.8 kg	50.2 lb	40.7 lb

START OF BOIL
Goldings 5% alpha-acid.

	400 g	365 g	13 oz	11 oz

DRY HOP (CASK)

	66 g	60 g	2.2 oz	1.8 oz

BREWING METHOD
- Pour on the whole quantity of water , and mash $\frac{1}{2}$ hour, then infuse for $2\frac{1}{2}$ hours.
- Run the liquor onto the hops previously infused in water.
- Boil the wort for 2 hours.
- Cool and pitch the yeast.
- When the beer has done working, ram the dry hops into the bung hole, plug and stand for 12 months

COMMENTS Obviously a second beer and maybe a third was mashed and made from the hops and I'm sure that the second run was still coming through at 1060. The beer from the first wort was reputed to keep as long as eight to ten years.

Appendix 1

Some brewing terms used in this book.

Acetification Turn to vinegar. Some bacteria can continue to oxidise ethanol to ethanoic acid, formerly called acetic acid, commonly called vinegar.

Acidity See pH.

Alkalinity Some salts have the ability to alter the pH of water. Calcium hydrogen carbonate $Ca(HCO_3)_2$ lifts the value above 7 (neutral) and is said to increase alkalinity.

Alpha acids Bittering compounds in hops.

Ambient temperature Temperature of the surroundings.

Amsinck Victorian Brewmaster, who recorded brews he did or was present at, faithfully.

Anaerobic Without oxygen, as applied to a yeast working in a fermentation.

Aeration Getting air into solution, in order to provide oxygen for aerobic fermentation. Nowadays effected with a pump and sterile filter or gas washer. See rousing.

Aerobic With oxygen, as applied to a yeast working in a fermentation.

Attenuate Convert the fermentable sugar to alcohol.

Back From buck or bucket. Any holder of liquid; e.g. Underback = container on the floor.

Barley The grain from which most European and US beers are made.

Beer styles The opinions of a self appointed few, who try to tell the rest of us, what a beer should be like; e.g. this book.

Bottom mashing Running the mash liquor in from underneath the goods.

Brewer Man who brews beer.

Brewster Woman who brews beer.

Burton Town in Middle England, famed for its pale ales and bitters, due to the high calcium sulphate content in the water.

Bushel Volume of malt, around 8 gallons.

$CaCO_3$ Chemical formula for calcium carbonate, which is formed when calcium hydrogen carbonate decomposes during boiling or brewing. If it is not removed prior to brewing, it may detrimentally affect the beer and mash efficiency. Many brewers choose to ignore its effects.

Caramelisation Decomposing sugars by removing hydrogen and oxygen atoms, leaving carbon. Hence the darker colour of caramel.

Cask hops Hops added to the cask in which the beer is maturing or conditioning. Also called dry hopping. They may nowadays be added during the primary or secondary fermentation and still be called cask hops, but shouldn't be. Cask hops provide aromatic oils without increasing the bittering substantially. See copper hopping.

Casking Filling beer into a cask or keg, usually in order to leave some solids behind as sediment and to preserve the beer.

Cleansing Scottish brewing term for racking off after fermentation and letting the yeast settle for a few days before further racking.

Cold break As the wort cools suspended and dissolved particles settle out to leave a clear wort. Called the cold break. (See hot break)

Copper Any vessel used for boiling or heating a liquid. Formerly often made from copper.

Copper hops Hops used to supply bittering, by boiling with the wort.

Courage London Brewery, founded in the 19th century.

Craft Brewers Home brewers who brew according to the brewing craft, rather than use easy-use kits of mainly dubious pedigree – as exemplified by the "Craft Brewing Association" the UK's home brewing organisation.

Dickens Charles Victorian writer, active in London, and famous for his social comment and record of Victorian life and habits.

Dry hop See cask hops

Durden Park Beer Circle Home Brewing Club in West London famous for their work on researching forgotten beers and praised by Michael Jackson as "Brewing Archaeologists." They have tracked down and researched old brewing records for over 20 years and their final version of 'Old British Beers and How to Brew Them' will be published soon.

EBC Method of assigning a number to help identify the colour (darkness) of a beer. The higher the number, the darker the beer.

EBU Method of assigning a number to help identify the bittering (as supplied by hops) of a beer. The higher the number, the more bitter the beer.

Enzymes Molecules capable of breaking down large starch or sugar molecules into fermentable maltose. Their effectiveness is controlled by temperature and pH. In beer brewing they are the diastase enzymes which are again divided into two types, alpha and beta, depending on the temperature and pH at which they best work. The protease are also important in brewing, as they break down sticky heavy protein molecules in poor quality malt. Enzymes are also called biological catalysts. They are essential in driving the chemical processes in all living things.

Export A beer strong enough in alcohol and bitter enough in hops to withstand the rigours of a long sea journey.

Extraction The amount of material converted into soluble compounds and removed from the malt. The extract is the wort.

Farnham Area near the town of that name on the Surrey Hampshire border, famous for its hops, which are no longer available under that name.

Fermentable Any sugar capable of being turned to alcohol by yeast.

FG Final gravity. Also called racking gravity. The density of the young beer, prior to being racked into casks for the last time. The material responsible for the FG being greater than 1.000 is used in the secondary fermentation and is responsible for conditioning.

Fuggles British hop, commonly used in IPAs and still available.

Goldings British hop, commonly used in IPAs and still available.

Goods The material (grist) in the mash tun.

Gravity Correct name is specific gravity. The density of a wort, divided by the density of water and expressed without the decimal point. E.g. 1050 is a wort of density $1.050g/cm^3$

Green malt Barley is allowed to germinate and then dried to form malt. The germinated but not yet dried barley is called green malt.

Grist Any cereal used to make beer, usually malted barley.

Grits Any cereal used as an additional starch source to malted barley, usually because it is much cheaper than malt, or because the malt nitrogen content is too high and low nitrogen grits artificially lower said figure. Also called adjuncts.

Gyle Nowadays usually taken to mean "a brew". Actually it meant the total volume of wort available for fermentation.

Gypsum Calcium Sulphate. See Burton.

HCO_3^- Hydrogen carbonate ion, almost always present in natural water as calcium hydrogen carbonate. This ion is unstable when heated and precipitates out as chalk, (calcium carbonate).

Hops Dried female flowers of the climber *humulus lupulus*. Used in beer since the 17th century for flavouring and for their preservative qualities.

Hot break Suspended particles in the wort collide and coagulate during boiling. They become big enough to settle out and the wort clears. This point is called the hot break. (See cold break)

Hygroscopic Many materials, including malt, have a great affinity for water. They are able to take water from the air and raise their own moisture level. This often leads to foodstuffs being quickly ruined. (See slack malt.)

India Pale Ale An export ale, sent to India and other destinations and also enjoyed in Britain. The modern beer is much weaker and lower in flavour than the 19th century version.

Isomerisation Changing the shape of a molecule, without altering the ratio of the atoms. The isomerised molecule may or may not have the same/similar properties to the precursor. In brewing the alpha acids present in the hop flower are isomerised by boiling and this increases their bittering properties.

Kedgeree Indian dish, excellent with IPA.

Keeping beers Beers strong enough or bitter enough to resist bacterial infection and so keep a long time. See Export.

L. s. d. Pounds, shillings and pence. The old non-decimal currency of the UK. The price per barrel sometimes in pounds, but more usually in shillings, was used to name a beer. E.g. sixty shilling beer, written 60/-.

Lactobacilli Bacteria able to convert sugars into lactic acid (sour milk). It is essential to protect the wort or young beer from lacto-bacilli. The high alcohol concentrations and hopping rates inhibit lac-tobacilli growth in IPA. They are effectively destroyed by dilute bleach solution, but will reappear (always).

Malt Cereal, usually barley, which has been germinated so that energy food converting enzymes are released, and then dried so that the enzymes are dormant and preserved for the brewer. The enzymes are reactivated by the mash.

March Latest winter month (in the Northern Hemisphere) in which beer should traditionally be brewed.

Mashing Stirring malt with water to activate the enzymes and convert starch to fermentable maltose sugar.

McCrorie James Member of Durden Park and an authority on histor-ical Scottish Beers, especially IPA and Majority Ales. Founder of the Craft Brewing Association, the UK's homebrewing organisation.

October Earliest winter month (in the Northern Hemisphere) in which beer should traditionally be brewed.

OG (Original Gravity) See also Starting Gravity. The gravity of a wort before pitching with yeast.

Pale malts Malt which has been carefully dried and hardly roasted, in order to preserve its pale colour and high enzyme activity. The palest modern malts are lager malt and in the 19th century, was white malt.

pH Hydrogen ion concentration expressed logarithmically. A measure of acidity or alkalinity, usually on a scale from 0-14. 0-6 is acidic, 7 is neutral, and 8-14 alkaline. For brewing purposes the pH of mash liquor should be 7-8 and during a mash and fermentation should fall to acidic, in the range 4.5-5.5. Brewers purchase narrow range (4-8) pH indicator papers. pH meters measure the hydrogen ion concen-tration directly but need a lot of TLC in order to work accurately. pH papers are probably a better buy for small brewers of pale ales. But even they, cheap as they are, are much of a waste of time, especially for darker worts, and especially as a good mash liquor and good malt always manage to hit the right pH for enzyme activity.

Pitch Add working yeast to a wort to ferment it.

Primary fermentation The most vigorous part of a fermentation, dur-ing which the maltose is converted to alcohol and carbon dioxide.

Pyrolisis Heating an organic molecule until only the carbon is left. E.g. burning food.

Rack Transfer from one vessel to another, usually with a view to leav-ing a sediment behind and preserving the beer or wort.

Rouse Stir to occlude oxygen and/or to keep the yeast working by preventing it settling or rising and becoming unavailable for fermen-tation.

Run off The first or second worts or the sparge liquor are removed from the goods by "running off."

Second mash Washing the maltose solution from the goods, by run-ning a fresh liquor charge onto the goods and infusing. Actually not a mash at all, but a wash process. Historically it was called mash due to the stirring action. (See sparging).

Secondary Fermentation A much slower fermentation of higher sugars to produce a variety of taste components. This takes place in a cask or bottle. It is referred to as maturation or conditioning.

SG Starting Gravity. See OG. Can also stand for specific gravity, depending on the context.

Set tap Run the wort off the grist.

Shive To put a bung into a cask. See spile.

Skimming Skimming the yeast head off a fermenting brew.

Slack(ed) Scottish term. To set the tap, i.e. to run the wort off the grist.

Slack malt Malt which has been allowed to take up water from the air after drying. (See hygroscopic)

Sodium metabisulphite Powerful sterilising agent. Decomposes to form sulphur dioxide gas, which will destroy enzyme activity in beer but can be useful outside the cask.

Sparge Running water through the goods, to extract the maltose solution, called wort. See second mash.

Spile Thin weak cask plugs, functioned as a safety valve. They are only noted when they were "not porous." This would indicate high attenuation before casking, i.e. the young beer was well flat and not much carbon dioxide was still to be expected. A porous spile allowed gas exchange. See shive.

Strike temperatures Temperature at which the grist is added to the mash liquor or vice versa.

Store Scottish word for a working active yeast.

Tap temperature Originally the temperature of the wort running out the tap. May be interpreted as the mash temperature when thinking modern day.

Torrefied Rude treatment of cereals, rendering them only fit for colouring and flavour, but not for extract.

Turning under, turning over See bottom mashing.

Ushers Famous Scottish brewery, celebrated for the quality of its beers. An English brewery of the same name also brewed some fine beers.

Victorian Adjective to describe things taking place during the reign of Queen Victoria, (1837-1901). Now taken to mean the last 60-70 years of the 19th century.

Vineous Description of beer if the alcohol has been allowed to oxidise to vinegar.

v/v Volume of alcohol in a given volume of beer. Usually expressed as a percentage.

w/v Weight of alcohol in a given volume of beer. Usually expressed as a percentage.

w/w Weight of alcohol in a given weight of beer. Usually expressed as a percentage. For all intents and purposes the same as w/v, the density of beer being practically $1.000g/cm^3$.

Yeast Micro-organism capable of converting sugars to alcohol and carbon dioxide.

Young beer Freshly fermented beer after the primary fermentation, but not conditioned. See secondary fermentation.

Younger's Famous Edinburgh brewery.

Appendix 2

Water treatment.

In recent years the hobby of home beer-making has seen many significant changes. No longer is it just a means of producing cheap alcohol. We have reached such a degree of sophistication and excellence that there can be little doubt that home brewed beers are the best beers!

The availability of top quality equipment and ingredients has put home brewers almost on a level playing field with their commercial counterparts. Now, however, the final piece of the jigsaw is to hand. You now have access to the professional brewing aids that can make a good beer great. By properly treating your water, feeding the yeast and using clarifiers that work, excellent beers are virtually guaranteed, whether you are a masher, extract brewer or quality kit maker. Please read on to find out the details.

WATER TREATMENT

As water is by far the main ingredient of beer, it is important that it is suitable for the purpose. Historically, beers were brewed to suit the water available, e.g. stouts and porters were produced primarily in London and Dublin where the water is high in carbonates, pale ales and bitters, however, were far more suited to the gypseous water of Burton-On-Trent.

With the advance of science it is now possible to brew most beer styles with any type of water providing it is correctly treated. To illustrate this we have broken down the procedure into three operations.

1. Filtration
Although most domestic water supplies are perfectly suited to brewing, they usually contain elements that are best removed. Foremost among these is chlorine, added to water for disinfectant purposes, but other substances such as sand, rust, polyphenols etc. also have a deleterious effect on the brewing process. Brewing beer with unfiltered water is leaving too much to chance! Most specialist home brew retailers will be able to offer a suitable water filter to remove these unwanted substances.

2. Adjustment of Carbonate Levels
In order to produce quality pale beers, the brewing liquor must

be low in carbonates as they prevent the correct mash pH from being achieved. Quality pale ales, bitters and lagers cannot be made with such water, so appropriate measures must be taken to correct its composition. Brupaks CRS (Carbonate Reducing Solution) is an acid blend which, when added to brewing liquor, reduces the level of carbonate without the need to boil. Darker beers can tolerate higher levels of carbonates.

3. Adjustment of Calcium Levels
Calcium is a very important mineral in the brewing process for its effect on mash and wort pH. Calcium chloride and calcium sulphate (gypsum) are used to lower the pH (increase the acidity), whereas, when brewing dark beers with soft water, calcium carbonate is sometimes added to balance the inherent acidity of the roasted grains. Brupaks Dry Liquor Salts (DLS) is a carefully controlled blend of inorganic salts designed to increase calcium levels and lower pH. When brewing pale ales and bitters it is usual to use both CRS and DLS to treat the liquor, as most water supplies have an excess of carbonate and insufficient calcium. For lager it is recommended that CRS be used in the mashing liquor to reduce carbonate, followed by careful additions of lactic acid to the mash tun for lowering the pH. An alternative to lactic acid is to incorporate some German acid malt in the grist. This special malt is used extensively in Germany in the production of high class lagers.

USING BRUPAKS WATER TREATMENT

Before you can start to treat your water you should first contact your water supply company and request the total alkalinity of your water in ppm. Unfortunately this is not as clear cut as it should be. Water authorities usually express alkalinity as HCO_3^- (hydrogen carbonate) whereas the brewing industry uses the traditional $CaCO_3$ (calcium carbonate). To use the tables below you will need to know the alkalinity expressed as $CaCO_3$. As you will probably have only the HCO_3^- value, you can convert it to $CaCO_3$ simply by dividing this figure by 1.22. From this figure it is possible to determine the required amounts of CRS and DLS to be added for all styles of beer. An average bitter or pale ale requires the water to have a total alkalinity of 30-50 ppm. and a calcium content of 180-220 ppm. If the total alkalinity of your water is below 50 ppm. you will not need to use CRS but will most probably need to increase the calcium with DLS.

Example: You are brewing a bitter and the total alkalinity of your water as $CaCO_3$ is 195 ppm. In order to bring it within

163

the target range of 30-50 ppm. you will need to reduce the alkalinity by 145-165 ppm. From the following table you can calculate the amount of CRS to be added. N.B. All brewing liquor should be treated with CRS, not just that used for mashing.

CRS in millilitres per litre

CRS	0.35	0.52	0.70	0.87	1.05	1.22	1.40	1.57	1.75
Alkalinity	-64	-96	-128	-160	-192	-224	-256	-288	-320

The table shows that to reduce the alkalinity by 160 ppm, CRS should be added at a rate of 0.87ml per litre. Thus for a standard 25 litre brew, which will probably require 30 litres of liquor, 30 x 0.87 = 26mls of CRS should be added. After adding CRS, several minutes standing time should be allowed to release the carbon dioxide produced by the neutralisation of the excess acid.

Now that the carbonate level has been adjusted, you have to correct the calcium content. Fortunately a close approximation of the amount of calcium present can be obtained by a simple piece of arithmetic:

Original alkalinity in ppm x 0.4 = Calcium in ppm

In the above example you have an original alkalinity of 195 ppm. Using the above formula the calcium content can be calculated as follows: 195 x 0.4 = 78 ppm.

A typical bitter requires a calcium content of 180-220 ppm. As you already have 78 ppm. you will need an extra 102-142 ppm. The quantity of DLS required can be ascertained from the table below.

DLS in grams per litre

DLS	0.1	0.2	0.3	0.4	0.5	0.6	0.7	0.8	0.9	1.0	1.1
Calcium	16	31	47	63	94	109	125	141	156	172	188

The table shows that in order to increase the calcium content by 125 ppm you will need to add 0.7 grams of DLS per litre.

When making a full mash brew, DLS should be added in two stages:

Stage 1. Weigh sufficient DLS to treat your mashing liquor (e.g. 10 litres x 0.7 = 7 grams). Mix DLS into the dry grains. This is most important as adding it to raw liquor will not affect the mash pH.

Stage 2. Weigh sufficient DLS to treat the balance of the total brewing liquor (e.g. 20 litres x 0.7 = 14 grams). Add to the wort at the commencement of the boil.

From the above information you should be able to treat almost any water to brew first class bitters and pale ales. Other styles of beer, however, require different levels of carbonate and calcium. These are the recommended alkalinity and calcium levels for the pale ales of the type IPA falls under.

Bitter and pale ale.   Alkalinity as $CaCO_3$ – up to 50 ppm. Calcium – 180 to 220 ppm.

WATER TREATMENT PRODUCTS

Brupaks supplies the following products for the treatment of brewing water. All of these products are available from good home brew shops throughout the UK.

Filterstream Water Filter. Manufactured by Sodastream. Excellent off-line filter with replaceable cartridges. Easily fitted, no plumbing required. Removes chlorine, polyphenols, heavy metals etc. Price around £40.00

Calcium Chloride Flakes. For simple calcium additions. Available in 500g packs.

Carbonate Reducing Solution (CRS). An acid blend that neutralises carbonates without the need to boil. Available in 250ml bottles.

Dry Water Treatment Salts. A carefully controlled blend of inorganic salts for precise treatment of brewing liquor. Available in 100g and 250g packs.

Gypsum (calcium sulphate). For simple calcium additions. Available in 250g packs.

Burton Water Crystals. A blend of calcium sulphate and magnesium sulphate intended to 'Burtonise' the liquor. Available in 250g packs.

Murphy's Water Treatment Product Information was kindly supplied by

Brupaks, 46-48 Colne Valley Business Park, Linthwaite, Huddersfield HD7 5QG. Tel: 01484 841116 Fax: 01484 841168 Email: brupaks@brupaks.com. www.brupaks.com

Author's Note: To blend salt additions properly, needs a balance accurate to 0.5g. Fortunately, these are now available for around £30, and are virtually indestructible. It will also come in handy for accurate hop additions.

Appendix 2a

Amsinck Water Analyses.

Water Comments from Amsinck.

- Soft water for brown beers, old ales especially where the malt is worked short.

- For running ales, hard water is best , the ale becomes ready immediately it is clear and is fuller in the mouth at the early stage.

- Brewers with sulphates, but devoid of carbonates are lucky. Calcium hydrogen carbonate $Ca(HCO_3)_2$ injures the flavour of the malt, especially when short worked, and hides the bitter of the hop. Every copperside operator must have an analysis of the water or he is working in the dark.

- All waters Amsinck used can produce an excellent beer. Calcium Sulphate $CaSO_4$ is supposed to be good for brewing. Amsinck differs. It is the system of brewing that is important.

- All water containing lime should be boiled overnight 15 minutes to precipitate the lime.

Remember: 1ppm = 1mg/l

Analysis 3. Burton Well

Component	Quantity grains/ imp. gal (ppm)	Comment
$CaCO_3$	15.5 (19)	Good for all ales,
$CaSO_4$	19 (24)	especially where the malt
$CaPO_4$		is worked up. Not suitable
FeCO	0.6 (1)	for brown beers.
$MgSO_4$	10 (12)	
$MgCO_3$	1.7 (2)	
K_2SO_4	7.7 (10)	
Na_2CO_3		
NaCl	10 (12)	
Silicic acid	0.79 (1)	

Analysis 5

Component	Quantity grains/ imp. gal (ppm)		Comment
$CaCO_3$	15.4	(19)	
$CaSO_4$	5.8	(7)	This liquor has produced
$CaPO_4$			splendid pale ale. There is
$FeCO_3$			too much carbonate
$FePO_4$			hardness, which hides
Organic	0.7	(1)	the bitter of the hop, a
$MgCO_3$	1.1	(1)	larger quantity is required.
K_2SO_4			Does not improve the
NO_3^--ion	4.5	(6)	flavour of the malt.
Cl—ion	4	(5)	
Silicic acid	1	(1)	

Analysis 9

Component	Quantity grains/ imp. gal (ppm)		Comment
$CaCO_3$			
$CaSO_4$	8.8	(11)	
Organic			
Mg nitrate & chloride	2.2	(3)	This liquor has particularly suited pale and fine strong
$FePO_4$			ales equal to any, and
$MgSO_4$			superior to most. There is
$MgCO_3$	4.2	(5)	a total absence of
K_2SO_4			carbonate hardness, thus
KCl	1	(1)	12lb (hops) will replace
NaCl	5	(6)	20lb, where carbonate
Silicic acid	1	(1)	hardness prevails.

Analysis 11

Component	Quantity grains/ imp. gal (ppm)	Comment
CO_3^{2-} from		Very good for pale ale and
Mg & Ca	26 .4 (33)	strong ales, a first class
$CaSO_4$	17 .6 (22)	production was made
Organic		from it. Very good for
$MgCl_2$	0 .8 (1)	brown beers.
$FePO_4$		
$MgSO_4$	25 .6 (32)	
$MgCO_3$		
K_2SO_4		
$Na2CO_3$		
NaCl	2 .2 (3)	
Silicic acid		

Appendix 3

Making White Malt

To make malt requires brewer's barley from the most recent harvest. Reject anything over one year old. There should be an assay available on the nitrogen content, which should fall within a precise narrow range. I don't get too excited about the assay, as we home brewers don't have to worry about getting a bit of protein haze in our beer, and anyway, the use of low nitrogen grits, or a little white sugar, will solve the protein problem if you are sensitive about haze.

The barley is steeped and aerated for several days, during which time it takes up water. It is then germinated and the germination terminated by drying at exactly the right moment. The dehydration stops further enzyme activity within the grain and once dry, the enzymes are reasonably stable to heat. The malt can then be roasted to give it colour. The trick with white malt, is not to roast it. It is dried at not much above room temperature, finished and then bagged up.

Continental lager malt is dried at around the right temperature but may be finished at around 60°C. I would finish white malt at 35-40°C.

The temperatures for steeping and germinating are exactly prescribed, and can usually only be maintained during the winter months. A heated shed would be ideal. Cellars are usually spot on for most of winter. I shall cheat a little in the future, and ask my local malting to sell me some green malt. That is malt, which has been germinated but not dried. The only problem with that is, one must work up the green malt immediately. It will not wait even a few hours once it is ready for drying.

Exact details of how to set up a home malting are to be found in *The Historical Companion to House-Brewing* by Clive La Pensée, available from CAMRA books on 01727 867201.

Getting round high nitrogen barley is dealt with in *The Craft of House-Brewing*, currently available from Montag Publications, 6, Minster Ave. Beverley HU17 0NL £9.95 including p+p, or from CAMRA Books.

Appendix 4

Suitable Yeasts

Dried yeast users must be sure to make up a working yeast starter several hours before it will be needed. Do take a good product and follow the maker's instructions or use one of the many excellent beer books available from your retailer. *The Craft of House-Brewing*, also available through CAMRA books gives exact details on starting a dried yeast and on propagating from a living one.

Dried yeast brands such as Gervin, Safale and Lalamand are totally reliable and will give you the necessary high degree of attenuation, which a genuine IPA requires.

Good homebrew retailers will also be able to supply Brewlab products, which are live yeasts. They have to be started according to the maker's instructions before use.

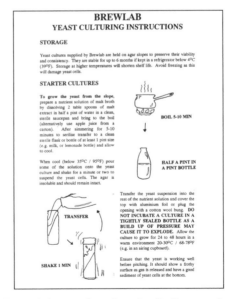

Brewlab instruction sheet for its live yeasts.

Appendix 5

Reprint of the Introduction to "India Beers,"
by Roberts. 1847 edition.

Although this book is designated the Scottish Ale-Brewer, and is a practical treatise on the art of brewing ales, according to the system practised in Scotland, it may not be deemed out of place to diverge so far from the proposed object, as to introduce an article on brewing beers for the India Market. This, I think, will not be unacceptable, but on the contrary may prove useful to those who wish to cultivate this branch of the export trade, in which many of our eminent brewers in Britain have been engaged for the last twenty years.

For a long period, up to about 1820, this trade was almost exclusively in the hands of one individual. It is impossible to know what suggested to Mr. Hodgson the idea of brewing for the India Market, but from the unrivalled fame his beers soon acquired, and which they retained during many years in India, we may infer that his system was based on sound principles. It is well known, that the orders Mr. Hodgson received, were fully as many as he could well execute. The high preservation in which his beers were uniformly found at the end of the voyage and their continuing sound during any reasonable length of time in so unfavourable a climate, justly entitled him to the confidence of the public: in fact, Hodgson's beer was as well known in India, and as highly appreciated, as is London porter all over the world.

Mr. Hodgson's successful career was a sufficient stimulus to induce others to enter the field, although a great disadvantage, having to compete with so eminent a name. However, notwithstanding those difficulties, competitors still persevered, and eventually some of them succeeded in obtaining a large portion of the trade, and for several years past almost all the breweries in the neighbourhood of large sea-ports have occasionally been at work for the India market.

Formerly, in Edinburgh, there was only one firm that brewed for India; now there are several. Of late, the greatest competition appears to have been carried out by two rival brewers at Burton-on-Trent, who still continue with spirit to vie with each other. The vast quantity which they export to the India market will be seen from the following quotations, from the advertisements which recently appeared in almost all the provincial papers in Great Britain, and which I take leave to introduce as an evidence of the extent of their trade in this article. As I notice it solely for this purpose, it would be out of place to make any comment on their correspondence; therefore , under A is Messrs. Allsop and Sons' statement and under B is that from Messrs. Bass and Co.

A From Oct. 1, 1842 to Oct 1843 inclusive	Hhds.	B From Oct. 1843 to Feb. 1 1844	Hhds.
Allsop	9499	Bass	6868
Bass	4800	Allsop	5786
		Hodgson	606

Whether this export business comes up to their expectation, it is not for me to judge, but this I may safely affirm, that many who have brewed for this particular market have had good cause to repent of doing so.

I possess a letter from Bombay, dated July 1845, in which the writer mentions no less than 800 hogsheads of ————'s beer turned into the harbour, and adds, that a great portion arrives in a bad state, consequently fetches, as he observed, "a mere song". This fact will not be doubted, when reference is made to a table I have given of the original gravities, ascertained by Partial Evaporation, of forty samples of beer made for the India market and home consumption, many of which will be seen to be miserably low. Even keeping beers for the home consumption, were they made from such low gravities as some to be found in this table, would certainly not stand over the summer. I may observe here, that several samples which I have now tested, have been to India and other foreign climates. The writer of the letter referred to adds, "that good sound beer always fetches its price in India."

India pale beer being so highly impregnated with the finest hops, has not only been appreciated in India as a refreshing beverage, but when used in moderation, is also considered as an excellent stomachic. So much is this the case, that when our countrymen returned home, they felt the want of their "Hodgson," and in consequence, it is more than probable that some of the influential among them urged the brewers to make a similar article for the home trade. They have done so, and their success has been beyond their expectations. This success no doubt, has been principally owing to the very favourable opinion entertained of its tonic qualities by several of our most eminent medical men, who have recommended it to their patients, as a strengthening, exhilarating, and wholesome beverage.

*What is called India Beer is now very generally used in Great Britain. Such being the case, and as we are likely to find from our relations in the East, a good market for this article, even in China, it is of the greatest importance to those who wish to compete with others, that they should acquire every information regarding the method of making those beers; and it must be evident, that to be put in possession of the original gravities and attenuations of the beers, of those who have been very successful, will accomplish a very essential point towards it. For this purpose I have examined, by Partial Evaporation, forty samples from the London, Scottish, Burton, and other English provincial brewers.

I have entered more fully into the introductory part of this article than I intended, and for which I trust my readers will excuse me.

Appendix 6

This is the Brewing Journal from Wm. Younger & Co. Edinburgh, Scotland. See Recipe 20, (historical), Younger's Export Ale of 1848.

	ATTENUATIONS.										DRY HOPS.		CLEANSINGS.									
Heat of Tun Room	Pitching Ht. & Gty.	1st. Morg.	1st. Evg.	2nd. Morg.	2nd. Evg.	3rd. Morg.	3rd. Evg.	4th. Morg.	4th. Evg.		Lbs.	Quality and Proportions.	Date.	Butts.	Hhds.	Barrels.	½ Barrels.	½ Hhds.	¼ Hhds.	Ale.	Remarks.	
		m 7 4pm									1007										106,832	2777
	59 50	61½ 45	64 36	69½ 26	71 20	72 14 / 70 13	67 12	63 12		Off 12th Clg B Bi Bull	73		12th		20 / 9	39 / 30				XPCa / P	4400	112
45	59 50	61½ 45	64 38	69½ 26 (Sk midl 57½)	72 20	72 13 / 70 13	67 12	63 12		good sl c fl												
					Sk 7.30am = 62½																	
	59 43	60 41	62 39	65 30	68 24	71 16 / 70 14	65 13	60 13		Off 13th Clg B Bi Bull	42		12th		30	47		30		H60/	4295	118
41	59 43	60 41	62 39	65 29	68 25	71 16 / 70 14	65 13	60 11		do do												
		m 7 8am																11.		ave 140/		
102	56 104	62½ 92	67½ 81	75 56	76 46	71 39	65 38	63 18		Off 13th Clg B good stgale fl Bull			13th					24	30	160/	1811	4
94 (54 57½ / 60 68)	56½ 96	62½ 83	67½ 72	75 50	75 41 (Sk 4pm = 50½)	71½ 36	64 35	63 35		Off 13th Clg B Bull good			13th		6			9 / 11	25 / 15	140/ / ave 120/	1789	4
				Sk 3pm = 56½																		
	59 43	64 34	66 28	70 19	71 16	68 13	63 12			Off 12th Clg B Bi Bull	46		12th			43	90		31 / 80/	H60/	4654	12
41	59 43	64 33	66 27	70 18	71 15	67½ 11	63 11			good sl c fl												
		m 7 noon		Sk 10.30am = 49½																		
70	58½ 72	62½ 64	65 57	72 41	71 35	65 33	61 33			Off 12th Clg B both Bull			12th					39	45	100/	2.200	5
48	59 50	61 46	63½ 40	68 30	69 25 (Sk 4.30pm = 55½)	66 21	62 20			Off 12th Clg B both good sl c fl			12th					59	20	60/	2.342	6
		m 7 4pm			Sk 4pm = 52½																	
	59 50	61 45	63 40	67½ 31	69 25	67 21	63 20			Off 12th Clg B Bull			12th		7			110	16	60/	4506	11
46	59 50	61 45	63 40	67½ 30	69 25	67 21	63 20			good sl c fl												
				Sk noon = 47½																		
32	59½ 34	62 32	63½ 27	67½ 18	68 13	65 11	62 10			Off 12th Clg B Bi both Bull	30		12th		10			34	30	50/	2283	6
27	60 29	61½ 28	63 25	66 17	67 12	65 8	62 6			Off 12th Clg B both good sl c fl			12th		30			3		II	2284	5
		39 fast																				
	58 74	59½ 71 (11am = 36½ 69.52)	62 67	Pumping 11 det.	69½ 43	67 22 / 66 19	62½ 17	60 16		Off 13th Clg B 1/8 Salicylic Bull	117		13th			117				XXXX	4 410	11
72	58 74	59½ 71	62 67	Pumping 16 det	69½ 43	67 23 / 66 20	62½ 17	60 16		good sl c fl												
											1315										141,806	368

Bibliography

Beer literature quoted in this work.

1. Amsinck G.S. *Practical Brewing. A series of fifty brewings in extens.* London 1868
2. Amsinck G.S. *Statistics Relating to the Brewing Trade* pp 21. London 1865
3. Brigg, Hough, & Stevens. *Malting and Brewing Science Vol. 1* Young, Chapman & Hall. London 1994
4. Dickens C. *The Old Curiosity Shop* Collins. London 1908
5. Harrison J. *Old British Beers and How To Make Them* Durden Park Beer Circle. 1991
6. James H. *The Art of Brewing India Pale Ale and Export Ale, Stock and Mild Ales, Porter and Stout* London 1865
7. Korzonas A. *Homebrewing Volume 1* Sheaf & Vine. Illinois 1997
8. La Pensée C.W. *The Craft of House-Brewing* Montag Publications. Beverley 1990
9. La Pensée C.W. *The Historical Companion to House-Brewing* Montag Publications. Beverley 1996
10. Loudon J.C. *An Encyclopedia of Cottage, Farm and Villa Architecture* 1833
11. Levesque J. *The Art of Brewing and Fermenting* Thomas Hurst. London 1854
12. Noonan G.J. *New Brewing Lager Beer* Brewer's Publications. Boulder 1996
13. Roberts W.H. *The Scottish Ale Brewer* Oliver & Boyd. Edinburgh 1838
14. Roberts W.H. *The Scottish Ale Brewer and Practical Maltster 3rd Edition* A. & C. Black. Edinburgh 1847
15. Sambrook P. *Country House Brewing in England 1500-1900* The Hambledon Press. London 1996
16. Tizard W.L. *Theory and Practice of Brewing* London 1850
17. *Domestic Brewing; a Hand Book for Families* New Library of Useful Knowledge. London 1839
18. *The Brewer. A familiar treatise on the art of brewing* William Loftus. London 1867
19. *The Family Cookery Book* William Nicholson & Sons. Wakefield

The CAMRA Books range of guides helps you search out the best in beer (and cider) and brew it at home too!

BUYING IN THE UK

All our books are available through bookshops in the UK. If you can't find a book, simply order it from your bookshop using the ISBN number, title and author details given below. CAMRA members should refer to their regular monthly newspaper What's Brewing for the latest details and member special offers. CAMRA books are also available by mail-order (postage free) from: CAMRA Books, 230 Hatfield Road, St Albans, Herts, AL1 4LW. Cheques made payable to CAMRA Ltd. Telephone your credit card order on 01727 867201.

BUYING OUTSIDE THE UK

CAMRA books are also sold in many book and beer outlets in the USA and other English-speaking countries. If you have trouble locating a particular book, use the details below to order with your credit card (or US$ cheque) by mail, email or fax (+44 1727 867670).

Carriage of £3.00 per book (Europe) and £6.00 per book (US, Australia, New Zealand and other overseas) is charged.

UK BOOKSELLERS

Call CAMRA Books for distribution details and book list. CAMRA Books are listed on all major CD-ROM book lists and on our Internet site: http://www.camra.org.uk

OVERSEAS BOOKSELLERS

Call or fax CAMRA Books for details of local distributors. Distributors are required for some English language territories. Rights enquiries (for non-English language editions) should be addressed to the managing editor.

HOMEBREW CLASSICS – THE SERIES

Price: £8.99

The Homebrew Classics series tells you everything you need to know about particular beer styles. You will discover the history behind the beer, the characters involved and the business of beer brewing in the era that created and enjoyed the particular beer style. Each book provides the background knowledge about ingredients and technique so that you can can reproduce the style authentically with your homebrew equipment.

In order to create this series CAMRA has brought together the talents of top home brewers and top beer writers to bring you both the technical knowhow and the knowledge of beer styles – their history, provenance and modern ingredients as commercially brewed.

Look out for the other titles in the series: Mild, Stout & Porter, Bitter and more.

BREW YOUR OWN REAL ALE AT HOME

by Graham Wheeler and Roger Protz
196 pages   Price: £8.99   ISBN 1-85249-138-8

This book contains recipes which allow you to replicate some famous cask-conditioned beers at home or to customise brews to your own particular taste. Conversion details are given so that the measurements can be used world-wide.

BREW CLASSIC EUROPEAN BEERS AT HOME

by Graham Wheeler and Roger Protz
196 pages   Price: £8.99   ISBN 1-85249-117-5

Keen home brewers can now recreate some of the world's classic beers. In your own home you can brew superb pale ales, milds, porters, stouts, Pilsners, Alt, Kolsch, Trappist, wheat beers, sour beers, even the astonishing fruit lambics of Belgium... and many more. Measurements are given in UK, US and European units, emphasising the truly international scope of the beer styles within.

HOME BREWING

by Graham Wheeler
240 pages   Price: £8.99   ISBN 1-85249-137-X

Recently redesigned to make it even easier to use, this is the classic first book for all home-brewers. While being truly comprehensive, Home Brewing also manages to be a practical guide which can be followed step by step as you try your first brews. Plenty of recipes for beginners and hints and tips from the world's most revered home brewer.

CAMRA'S GOOD CIDER GUIDE

by David Matthews
400 pages   Price: £9.99   ISBN 1-85249-143-4

CAMRA's guide to real cider researched anew for the new Millennium and now with features on cider around the world – North America, France, Spain.

CAMRA'S LONDON PUBS GUIDE

by Lynne Pearce
256 pages   Price: £9.99   ISBN 1-85249-164-7

Real ale and great food in London pubs with stories to tell. What could be better? This is your guide to finding excellent real ale in the capital. The book provides detailed descriptions of CAMRA's top 250 London pubs, together with street level maps and a selection of illustrations.

Pubs are listed with opening times, travel details, food arrangements, parking, disabled and children's facilities indicated. Plus the all-important range of beers.

CELLARMANSHIP

by Ivor Clissold
144 pages   Price: £6.99   ISBN 1-85249-126-4

This book explains every aspect of running a good cellar and serving a great pint of real ale which does both pub and brewer proud. It's a must have book for all professionals in the drinks trade, for all those studying at college to join it, and for all those who need to tap a cask of real ale for a party or beer festival.

CAMRA DICTIONARY OF BEER

edited by CAMRA
154 pages   Price: £7.99   ISBN 1-1-85249-158-2

This newly compiled dictionary contains thousands of definitions related to beer. The comprehensive descriptions and cross-referencing make this a unique specialist dictionary.

JOIN CAMRA

If you like good beer and good pubs you could be helping to fight to preserve, protect and promote them. CAMRA was set up in the early seventies to fight against the mass destruction of a part of Britain's heritage.

The giant brewers are still pushing through takeovers, mergers and closures of their smaller regional rivals. They are still trying to impose national brands of beer and lager on their customers whether they like it or not, and they are still closing down town and village pubs or converting them into grotesque 'theme' pubs.

CAMRA wants to see genuine free competition in the brewing industry, fair prices, and, above all, a top quality product brewed by local breweries in accordance with local tastes, and served in pubs that maintain the best features of a tradition that goes back centuries.

As a CAMRA member you will be able to enjoy generous discounts on CAMRA products and receive the highly rated monthly newspaper *What's Brewing*. You will be given the CAMRA members' handbook and be able to join in local social events and brewery trips.

To join, complete the form below and, if you wish, arrange for direct debit payments by filling in the form overleaf and returning it to CAMRA. To pay by credit card, contact the membership secretary on (01727) 867201.

Full membership £14; Joint (living partners') membership £17; Single under 26 £8; Joint under 26 membership £11; retired over 60, student, unemployed £8; Joint retired over 60 £11; UK/EU Life membership £168
Please delete as appropriate:
I/We wish to become members of CAMRA.
I/We agree to abide by the memorandum and articles of association of the company.
I/We enclose a cheque/p.o. for £   (payable to CAMRA Ltd.)

Name(s)

Address

Postcode

Signature(s)

CAMRA Ltd., 230 Hatfield Road, St Albans, Herts AL1 4LW

Instruction to your Bank or Building Society to pay by Direct Debit

Please fill in the whole form using a ball point pen and send it to:

Campaign for Real Ale Ltd,
230 Hatfield Road,
St. Albans,
Herts
AL1 4LW

Originator's Identification Number

| 9 | 2 | 6 | 1 | 2 | 9 |

Reference Number

| | | | | | | | | | | | | | | | | |

Name of Account Holder(s)

Bank/Building Society account number

| | | | | | | | |

Branch Sort Code

| | | | | | |

Name and full postal address of your Bank or Building Society

To The Manager   Bank/Building Society

Address

Postcode

FOR CAMRA OFFICIAL USE ONLY

This is not part of the instruction to your Bank or Building Society

Membership Number

Name

Postcode

Instructions to your Bank or Building Society
Please pay CAMRA Direct Debits from the account detailed on this instruction subject to the safeguards assured by the Direct Debit Guarantee. I understand that this instruction may remain with CAMRA and, if so, will be passed electronically to my Bank/Building Society

Signature(s)

Date

Banks and Building Societies may not accept Direct Debit instructions for some types of account

- -

This guarantee should be detached and retained by the Payer.

The Direct Debit Guarantee

- This Guarantee is offered by all Banks and Building Societies that take part in the Direct Debit Scheme. The efficiency and security of the Scheme is monitored and protected by your own Bank or Building Society.

- If the amounts to be paid or the payment dates change CAMRA will notify you 10 working days in advance of your account being debited or as otherwise agreed.

- If an error is made by CAMRA or your Bank or Building Society, you are guaranteed a full and immediate refund from your branch of the amount paid.

- You can cancel a Direct Debit at any time by writing to your Bank or Building Society. Please also send a copy of your letter to us.